Parque Natural
del Islote de Lobos
Isla de
Lobos

Corralejo

El Cotillo

**Parque Natural
de las Dunas
de Corralejo**

Lajares

Fuerteventura

Villaverde

La Oliva

399
Montaña Tindaya

Monumento a
Don Miguel de Unamuno

Ecomuseo de
La Alcogida

Puerto
del Rosario

Órzola

*Caleta del
Mojón Blanco*

a de
rdes

Jameos
del Agua

Arrieta

Charco
del Palo

Betancuria

Antigua

Vega de
Río Palma

Caleta de
Fuste

Pájara

*Malpaís
Grande*

FUERTEVENTURA

Las
Playitas

*Oasis
Park*

Jandía

0   5 km

0   3 miles

TWINPACK
Lanzarote and Fuerteventura

EMMA GREGG

If you have any ~~~~ a book or
or suggestions ~~~~
you can con~~~~
Twinpacks@~~~~

4 JAN 2023

AA Publishing
Find out more about AA Publishing and the wide
range of services the AA provides by visiting our
website at theAA.com/bookshop

~~~~t our website
~~~~ks at **https:**

~~~~ningham
Council

How to Use This Book

KEY TO SYMBOLS

✚ Map reference

✉ Address

☎ Telephone number

🕐 Opening/closing times

🍴 Restaurant or café

🚈 Nearest rail station

🚌 Nearest bus route

⛴ Nearest ferry route

♿ Facilities for visitors with disabilities

❓ Other practical information

▷ Further information

ℹ Tourist information

✋ Admission charges: Expensive (over €10), Moderate (€5–€10), and Inexpensive (€5 or less)

★ Major Sight ★ Minor Sight

👣 Walks 🚐 Drives

🛍 Shops

🎵 Entertainment and Activities

🍽 Restaurants

This guide is divided into four sections

• **Essential Lanzarote and Fuerteventura:** An introduction to the islands and tips on making the most of your stay.

• **Lanzarote and Fuerteventura by Area:** We've broken the islands into three areas, and recommended the best sights, shops, activities, restaurants, entertainment and nightlife venues in each one. Suggested walks and drives help you to explore.

• **Where to Stay:** The best hotels, whether you're looking for luxury, budget or something in between.

• **Need to Know:** The info you need to make your trip run smoothly, including getting about by public transport, weather tips, emergency phone numbers and useful websites.

Navigation In the Lanzarote and Fuerteventura by Area chapter, we've given each area its own colour, which is also used on the locator maps throughout the book and the inside front cover map.

Maps The fold-out map accompanying this book is a comprehensive map of Lanzarote and Fuerteventura. The grid on this fold-out map is the same as the grid on the locator maps within the book. The grid references to these maps are shown with capital letters, for example A1. The grid references to the town plans are shown with lower-case letters for example a1.

Contents

**ESSENTIAL LANZAROTE
AND FUERTEVENTURA** 4–18

Introducing Lanzarote
  and Fuerteventura
A Short Stay in Lanzarote
  and Fuerteventura 6–7
Top 25 8–9
Out and About 10–11
Shopping 12
Lanzarote and Fuerteventura
  by Night 13
Eating Out 14
Restaurants by Cuisine 15
If You Like... 16–18

**LANZAROTE AND
FUERTEVENTURA
BY AREA** 19–106
NORTHERN LANZAROTE 20–46

Area Map 22–23
Sights 24–38
Walk 39
Drive 41
Shopping 42
Entertainment
  and Activities 42–43
Restaurants 44–46

**CENTRAL AND SOUTHERN
LANZAROTE** 47–84

Area Map 48–49
Sights 50–70
Walks 71–72
Drives 73–74
Shopping 76
Entertainment
  and Activities 76–79
Restaurants 81–84

FUERTEVENTURA 85–106

Area Map 86–87
Sights 88–100
Drive 101
Shopping 102
Entertainment
  and Activities 102–105
Restaurants 105–106

WHERE TO STAY 107–112

Introduction 108
Budget Hotels 109
Mid-Range Hotels 110–111
Luxury Hotels 112

NEED TO KNOW 113–125

Planning Ahead 114–115
Getting There 116–117
Getting Around 118–119
Essential Facts 120–121
Language 122–123
Timeline 124–125

CONTENTS

Introducing Lanzarote and Fuerteventura

Lanzarote and Fuerteventura, close to the Moroccan coast, receive plenty of fine weather but there's far more to these subtropical islands than sun-drenched beaches: expect stunning volcanic land-scapes, avant-garde art and world-class watersports.

The easternmost of the Canary Islands, Lanzarote and Fuerteventura are geographically far nearer to Africa than to Europe. However, while some of their landscapes have a distinctly North African look—think mighty dunes and oasis-like villages of whitewashed, palm-shaded houses—culturally they lean firmly toward 'the Peninsula', the local term for mainland Spain.

Both islands used to make ends meet through agriculture and fishing. Today, tourism is a much bigger money-spinner but a few farmers keep their unusual, desert-adapted customs alive: Fuerteventura has large, covered tomato fields, while Lanzarote has cactus plantations and volcanic vineyards. The farmers and fishermen now share the islands with holidaymakers, who arrive by the planeload, and with retirees from Spain, Britain and Germany who spend all or part of the year here.

Lanzarote's determination to preserve as much as possible of its aesthetic and cultural heritage while reaping the benefits of mass tourism has made it one of the most attractive of the Canary Islands. Its modern developments, though sprawling, are low-rise, and mostly confined to the resorts, all of which are family-friendly. Its traditional inland villages and dramatic lava-strewn landscapes have survived more or less intact; these, along with striking gardens and architectural installations, encourage visitors to explore.

If all you want from your holiday is a comfortable hotel and a few great restaurants, Lanzarote and Fuerteventura will certainly fit the bill, but they're excellent for active breaks, too. If you've always wanted to learn to windsurf, this is the perfect place to get started, while if you'd like to have a go at scuba diving or kitesurfing, experts are on hand to show you the ropes.

Facts + Figures

- **Lanzarote welcomes over 1.8 million visitors each year, and Fuerteventura, over 1.4 million.**
- **Lanzarote has been a UNESCO Biosphere Reserve since 1993.**

WHAT'S COOKING?

There hasn't been a hint of an eruption on Fuerteventura for millennia, but Lanzarote's now-dormant volcanoes blew their top relatively recently, in 1824. In Timanfaya National Park, the temperature just beneath the surface is hot enough to cook a chicken.

THE MANRIQUE EFFECT

Lanzarote's most influential individual, César Manrique (1919–1992), inspired a conservation code that remains in force today. Strict planning restrictions help preserve the island's architectural integrity: most buildings are white and traditional in style. Balconies, doors and windows must be green, blue or brown, and billboards are banned.

MIND THE GOAT

All over Fuerteventura, warning triangles alert drivers to the hazard of leaping deer—an animal entirely absent from the island. Free-ranging goats, however, are plentiful. It turns out that the EU couldn't supply a standard road sign meaning 'danger: goats', so the authorities had to settle for the closest approximation.

A Short Stay in Lanzarote and Fuerteventura

DAY 1: LANZAROTE

Morning Make your way to the **Fundación César Manrique** (▷ 26–27) near Tahiche just north of Arrecife, for a fascinating insight into what made the great architect and thinker tick. You need to allow a couple of hours to explore Manrique's intriguingly designed former home and admire the inspirational paintings, photography and sculpture on display. Stay a while longer and relax in the garden with its stunning Manrique mural, evocative of the work of Picasso and Miró. Make sure you don't miss the colourful *juguete del viento* (wind mobile) at FCM, and the large silver one outside on the Cruce César Manrique roundabout, as you hop on the bus to **Arrecife** (▷ 50–51).

Lunch Choose a spot with a good view at **La Puntilla** (▷ 84), beside Arrecife's peaceful lagoon El Charco de San Ginés; it is ideal for a light lunch of salad, tortilla or grilled fish and a cold beer. For a treat try the langoustines.

Afternoon Take a long leisurely stroll around the El Charco de San Ginés, stopping to admire the Iglesia de San Ginés, and dropping in at the newly restored marketplace, La Recova. Then, continue along the city's pleasant seafront promenade. If you're ready for more modern art, backtrack to MIAC in the **Castillo de San José** (▷ 52) at the east end of town. But if you'd rather go shopping, aim for Calle León y Castillo, where you can lose an hour or so endulging in retail therapy.

Dinner For a memorable dinner, treat yourself to a table at the **Castillo de San José** (▷ 82) or **Altamar** (▷ 81) at the Gran Hotel.

Evening Then, if it's the weekend, you can get set to dance the night away with the locals at one of the clubs on Calle José Antonio.

DAY 2: FUERTEVENTURA

Morning Start the day in the Old Town district of **Corralejo** (▷ 90–91) with an invigorating dip in the sparkling sea from Playa La Clavellina. To get here, turn off the high street, Avenida Nuestra Señora del Carmen, at Calle Churruca. After your swim, reward yourself with a *café con leche* or a slap-up breakfast on the beachside deck at **The Point** (▷ 106).

Mid-morning Pick up a *línea* 8 bus, bound for Villaverde and La Oliva. After a short journey through the stark inland landscape and the smart little village of **Villaverde** (▷ 100) with its hilltop windmills, jump off at the historic town of **La Oliva** (▷ 92). Admire the imposing lava-and-whitewash church, Iglesia de Nuestra Señora de la Candelaria, and visit La Casa de los Coroneles, the one-time residence of the island's military governors. Then take a look around La Cilla, which hosts a small exhibition of agricultural history.

Lunch Backtrack a couple of kilometres, by bus or on foot, to the southern outskirts of Villaverde for a lunch of country fare at **Mahoh** (▷ 106), or head into the village for tapas at **Casa Marcos** (▷ 105).

Afternoon Return to Corralejo Old Town for a stroll along the seafront promenade and stop for coffee at a suitable spot.

Evening Settle yourself down for a waterside aperitif at the **Antiguo Café del Puerto** (▷ 102), then move on to **Tío Bernabé** (▷ 106) for a rousing Canarian dinner, or, for something more intimate, take a table at **Bodeguita El Andaluz** (▷ 105). Round off the night at **Blue Rock** (▷ 102) or **Music Box** (▷ 104).

Top 25

TOP
25

► ► ►

Arrecife ▷ 50–51
Capital of Lanzarote, a coastal city with an authentically Spanish atmosphere.

Betancuria ▷ 88 This picturesque little village dates back to the early days of conquest.

Castillo de San José ▷ 52 Arrecife's stocky fort houses an art museum and a stylish restaurant.

Yaiza ▷ 65 Pretty little village, perched between the Rubicón desert and Timanfaya.

Valle de la Geria ▷ 66–67 One of the most unusual wine regions on earth.

Teguise ▷ 34–35 A graceful old town that is a delightful spot for a leisurely lunch.

Punta de Papagayo ▷ 64 Desert wilderness dotted with lovely sandy coves.

Playa Grande ▷ 62–63 This huge beach has plenty of room for the many holidaymakers who head here.

Playa Blanca ▷ 60–61 Growing fast, but still Lanzarote's most pleasant coastal resort.

Roque de Infierno
Isla de Montaña Clara
La Gracio
El Río
Mirado del Rí

Lanzarote
La Isleta

NORTHERN LANZAROTE 20–46

Jardín de Cactus

Museo Agrícola El Patio
Centro de Visitantes e Interpretación
Monumento al Campesino
Teguise
Parque Nacional de Timanfaya
El Golfo
Valle de la Geria
Fundación César Manriq
Castillo San José
Yaiza
Arrecife

CENTRAL AND SOUTHERN LANZAROTE 47–84
Playa Grande

Playa Blanca
Punta de Papagayo

Península

Península de Jandía ▲ ▷ 93 Home to the best beaches in the Canaries, with amazing windsurfing.

Parque Natural de las Dunas de Corralejo ▷ 94–95 Dazzling dunes meet sparkling sea.

Parque Nacional de Timanfaya ▷ 58–59 The craters and lava fields of Lanzarote are unmissable.

ESSENTIAL LANZAROTE AND FUERTEVENTURA TOP 25

8

These pages are a quick guide to the Top 25, which are described in more detail later. Here they are listed alphabetically, and the tinted background shows which area they are in.

Centro de Visitantes e Interpretación ▷ 53 Learn about volcanoes in this informative museum.

Corralejo ▷ 90–91 A little tatty but lots of fun, this is one of Fuerteventura's most popular resorts.

Cueva de los Verdes ▷ 24 Trek deep into a mighty lava tube and admire its chambers.

Fundación César Manrique ▷ 26–27 The former home of this great artist, now a gallery.

El Golfo ▷ 54 The surreal coastal lagoon that inspired film-maker Almodóvar.

La Graciosa ▷ 32 For the ultimate in peace and quiet, make an escape to this arid island.

Isla de Lobos ▷ 89 Cruise over from Corralejo, or take a diving trip to explore intriguing lava reefs.

Jameos del Agua ▷ 28–29 An oasis in the volcanic landscape.

Jardín de Cactus ▷ 30–31 Plants arranged as art objects in a wonderful Manrique creation.

Mirador del Río ▷ 33 Enjoy a drink while you marvel at the panoramic views of La Graciosa.

La Oliva ▷ 92 Once the capital of Fuerteventura, now a quiet little place with traces of its noble past.

Museo Agrícola El Patio ▷ 56 Find out about Lanzarotean life before the advent of tourism.

Monumento al Campesino ▷ 55 Striking sculpture celebrating Lanzarote's pastoral heritage.

Isla de Lobos

Corralejo

Parque Natural de las Dunas de Corralejo

La Oliva

Cueva de los Verdes
Jameos del Agua

Betancuria

FUERTEVENTURA 85–106

Fuerteventura

andía

ESSENTIAL LANZAROTE AND FUERTEVENTURA TOP 25

◀ ◀ ◀

9

Out and About

The eastern Canaries' bright, breezy climate and wide open landscapes seem to spur on the superfit—and many of the less actively inclined, too. The sunny, dry and breezy conditions are good for running, cycling, hiking, sailing and windsurfing, as well as just switching off and relaxing on the beach.

Life's a Beach

Not long ago, fishermen would pull up their boats in the sheltered coves of Puerto del Carmen, Playa Blanca and Corralejo to unload the day's catch. Today, the same coves belong wholly to tourism, their fringes developed and their beaches enhanced with pale, attractive sand. These are among the most popular and convenient holiday beaches on the islands. The islands also retain a few wild, unspoilt beaches however, most notably on Lanzarote's Punta de Papagayo (▷ 64), and, on Fuerteventura, in the Parque Natural de las Dunas de Corralejo (▷ 94–95) and the Península de Jandía (▷ 93). To enjoy these to the full, you'll need to bring your own supplies of food and water, some shade and, on the breeziest days, a windbreak.

Windsurfing Mecca

Fuerteventura is an essential stop on the global windsurfing circuit, with Lanzarote not too far behind. Both host international tournaments during the summer. The key destination is Fuerteventura's Playa de Sotavento (▷ 93). This beautiful area is undeveloped, apart from

EXTREME ATHLETICS

If you like pushing yourself to the limit, you'll find yourself in good company—scores of athletes visit the islands to pedal or pound their way up its volcanic inclines. The more rugged tracks offer challenging conditions for cross-country running, while the inland roads are excellent for cycling, with spectacular views en route. For the truly hardcore, the supreme test is the Lanzarote Ironman (▷ panel, 77), an all-day swimming, cycling and running event.

The islands abound with soft, sandy beaches, and the colourful sails of windsurfers

a hotel, the Sol Meliá Gorriones (▷ 111), incorporating Pro Center René Egli (▷ 104), one of the most famous windsurfing bases in the world.

Explore the Ocean
If the idea of a yacht charter or a leisurely catamaran cruise floats your boat, head for Catlanza, located in both Puerto Calero (▷ 77) and Corralejo (▷ 104). These, along with Marina Rubicón (▷ 79), are also home to scuba diving outfits that run training courses in safe, shallow waters, and take experienced divers out by boat to explore interesting lava reefs, caves and wrecks.

Ride a Board
Both surfing and kitesurfing are growing sports on both islands. Ridges of submerged lava lie offshore to the northwest, particularly near La Santa (▷ 70) and Famara (▷ 43), ready to whip up a swell that's demanding enough to tax champions.

Best Foot Forward
Lanzarote's south and east coast paths are perfect for a leisurely stroll. Both islands are also popular with serious hikers: inland, paths aren't marked but the landscapes are so open that with a good map, water and sun protection it's hard to go wrong. For a unique perspective on Lanzarote's volcanoes, it's well worth joining a guided hike in Timanfaya National Park (▷ 72).

Varied landscapes offer all kinds of exciting activities from boat trips and kitesurfing to hiking

FINDING PEACE AND QUIET

While the main resorts on both islands can be noisy and crowded in the peak holiday season, it's easy enough to escape the crowds, particularly if you have your own transport. Both islands have nature reserves in which rare bird and plant species flourish, and both have wild, empty expanses of *malpaís* (volcanic badlands), parts of which can be explored by road or on foot. Both also have undeveloped stretches of coast, particularly on the windy, western shores.

Shopping

You won't find giant department stores on Lanzarote and Fuerteventura; instead, the islands have a good scattering of independents, designer and electrical outlets. Many museums sell the work of local artisans, and several towns have lively *mercadillos*, markets that mostly sell crafts and gifts.

Little Luxuries

Local specialties that you'll see everywhere include aloe vera products, jars of *mojo* (garlic sauce), decorative ceramic tiles and jewellery made from black lava beads, often combined with lime green olivina, a semi-precious volcanic stone. On Lanzarote look out for specialist shops selling souvenirs featuring César Manrique's distinctive graphics. Arrecife, Puerto Calero, Playa Blanca, Puerto del Rosario and Morro Jable have a few shops selling fashions from Spanish and international designers, and you'll see surf gear everywhere. Teguise has several fabulous gallery shops, as well as the biggest of the weekly *mercadillos* (▷ 34–35).

Bargain Buys

Lanzarote and Fuerteventura are sometimes mistakenly referred to as duty-free islands; in fact the local sales tax is simply lower, at 5 per cent, making many branded goods cheaper than they would be in the rest of the EU. Bear in mind that there are limits on what you can take home without paying duty on arrival (▷ 120). In the past, visitors have been caught out by shops selling electrical goods that transpire to be fakes, or have invalid guarantees.

WINE FROM LA GERIA

Lanzarotean wine, which is produced from grapes grown in volcanic gravel, is a talking point, and as it's hard to obtain outside the island, it makes a great purchase. Bought direct from the wineries, where your purchases will be packed in boxes, even the best vintages are reasonably priced. For a small charge you can taste the wines before you buy.

The Sunday market at Teguise on Lanzarote has a cornucopia of local crafts for you to buy

Lanzarote and Fuerteventura by Night

On Lanzarote and Fuerteventura nightlife comes in two distinct varieties: In the resorts a lively cabaret and bar scene caters for the tourist trade, while in the other towns and villages the locals socialize in restaurants, cafés and urban dance bars. Come fiesta time, everyone celebrates with parades and all-night merriment.

Resort Bars and Clubs

As a holiday destination, the eastern Canaries don't set out to attract party-mad teens and twentysomethings, concentrating instead on families and retirees. There's no shortage of friendly bars, and the large hotels all lay on entertainment, from traditional musicians to variety acts, but the dance scene is very low-key compared to the all-out megaclubs of the youth-oriented Mediterranean resorts. The busiest resort is Puerto del Carmen.

Local Scene

As in mainland Spain, there's a big overlap between restaurants, cafés, bars, tapas bars, bodegas (wine bars) and clubs. Some places cover several bases, opening early, serving food and drinks of all descriptions, welcoming families until very late in the evening, and turning up the volume later on. There are also a few after-dark venues that don't open their doors until 11pm or midnight, and don't close before dawn. To party with the locals, head for Arrecife or Puerto del Rosario on a Friday or a Saturday night.

FIESTA!

At fiesta time, the islanders really push the boat out—the packed calendar of Catholic festivals is marked by solemn processions, usually followed by much light-hearted may-hem. For visitors, the Fiestas del Carmen and San Ginés (▷ 114) celebrations in summer are colourful to watch, but the most fun of all is to be had during carnival time in February—especially if you deck yourself out in fancy dress and join in.

Neon signs light up the evening sky as things hot up in Puerto del Carmen, Lanzarote

Eating Out

If you were to stick to the resorts, you might wrongly conclude that the restaurant scene is pretty bland. Try the inland towns and villages as well—that's where the fires of culinary creativity burn brightest. Most restaurants welcome children, and everyone dresses up a little in the evenings.

Canarian Cooking

Classic Canarian cooking consists of tasty peasant food. Fish and seafood, of course, are principal ingredients, served grilled, fried, or in a stew such as *sancocho* (with potatoes and chickpeas) or *cazuela canaria* (fish and octopus casserole). Grilled or slow-roasted kid, rabbit and pork also feature. New potatoes boiled in their skins and served with *mojo verde* (garlic and coriander sauce) or *mojo rojo* (with chilli) are a favourite accompaniment. The best traditional restaurants are inland but even in the resorts, there are gems to be uncovered— you just need to know where to look.

International Cuisine

The resort restaurants offering menus covering everything from stroganoff to pizza have their place, but by trying to please everyone many settle for mediocrity overall. For gorgeous non-Canarian cuisine try one of the specialists: Agua Viva (▷ 81), Taberna Strelitzia (▷ 84) and Caserío de Mozaga (▷ 82) are great for French-inspired cooking; Casa Siam (▷ 82) is a superb Thai; and Emmax (▷ 83) serves brilliant modern Italian.

LOCAL TIPPLES

Lanzarote's *malvasía* wine is justly famous, even though the vineyards of La Geria are so 'boutique' that their bottles rarely leave the island, except in visitors' hand luggage. Many restaurant wine lists feature crisp local whites and fruity Moscatels alongside mainland Riojas and Ribera del Dueros, including top-ranking Reservas. For an after-dinner treat, try a shot of *ron miel*, a delicious honey rum: Cuarenta y Tres is the most popular brand.

Both Lanzarote and Fuerteventura offer an array of good places to eat in beautiful settings

Restaurants by Cuisine

There are restaurants, cafés, bodegas and bars to suit all tastes and budgets on Lanzarote and Fuerteventura. For a more detailed description of each of our recommendations, see Lanzarote and Fuerteventura by Area.

FINE DINING

LANZAROTE
Agua Viva (▷ 81)
Altamar (▷ 81)
Amura (▷ 81)
Aromas Yaiza (▷ 81)
Casa Roja (▷ 82)
Caserío de Mozaga (▷ 82)
La Casona de Yaiza (▷ 82)
Castillo de San José (▷ 82)
Don Antonio (▷ 105)
La Graciosa (▷ 45)
Lilium (▷ 83)
Mesón Tiagua (▷ 83)

FUERTEVENTURA
La Vaca Azul (▷ 106)

INTERNATIONAL

LANZAROTE
La Cabaña (▷ 82)
Casa Siam (▷ 82)
Domus Pompei (▷ 45)
Emmax (▷ 83)
Ikarus (▷ 45)
Mesón La Jordana (▷ 45)
Mezza Luna (▷ 84)
Neptuno (▷ 45)
Oscar's (▷ 45)
Quintin's (▷ 84)
Taberna Strelitzia (▷ 84)
El Tomate (▷ 84)
Vesubio (▷ 46)

FUERTEVENTURA
La Cancela (▷ 105)
Sidrería la Cabaña
    Asturiana (▷ 106)

LIGHT BITES

LANZAROTE
Bodegón de las Tapas
    (▷ 82)
La Bodeguita del Medio
    (▷ 44)
Café Jaleo (▷ 44)
El Chiringuito Casa García
    (▷ 44)
El Chupadero (▷ 83)
La Galería (▷ 45)
Los Helechos (▷ 45)
El Pastelito (▷ 46)
Pintxos y Tapas (▷ 84)

FUERTEVENTURA
The Point (▷ 106)

SPANISH

LANZAROTE
Acatife (▷ 44)
Almacén de la Sal (▷ 81)
Amanacer (▷ 44)
Bodega (▷ 81)
La Bodega de Santiago
    (▷ 81)
La Bodega de Uga
    (▷ 81)
El Bodegón los Conejeros
    (▷ 82)
Las Brasas (▷ 44)
Casa Emiliano (▷ 82)
Casa García (▷ 44)
Charco Viejo (▷ 44)
El Charcón (▷ 44)
Costa Azul (▷ 83)
Déjà Vu (▷ 83)
El Diablo (▷ 83)

El Horno de la Aguela
    (▷ 83)
Mar Azul (▷ 83)
Mesón de la Frontera
    (▷ 45)
O' Botafumeiro (▷ 84)
Patio Canario (▷ 46)
Perla del Atlántico (▷ 46)
Puerto Bahía (▷ 84)
Punta Fariones (▷ 46)
La Puntilla (▷ 84)
Restaurante Sol (▷ 46)
El Risco (▷ 46)
Taberna del Puerto (▷ 84)
La Tegala (▷ panel, 84)
Terraza Playa (▷ 84)
Las Tres Lunas (▷ 46)
El Varadero (▷ 46)
Villa Toledo (▷ 46)

FUERTEVENTURA
Bodeguita El Andaluz
    (▷ 105)
Casa Marcos (▷ 105)
Casa Santa María (▷ 105)
El Horno (▷ 106)
La Laja (▷ 106)
Mahoh (▷ 106)
Posada de San Borondón
    (▷ 106)
Roque de los Pescadores
    (▷ 106)
Tío Bernabé (▷ 106)

If You Like...

However you'd like to spend your time in Lanzarote and Fuerteventura, these ideas should help you plan the perfect visit. Each suggestion is cross-referenced to a fuller write-up elsewhere in the book

SHOPPING FOR CRAFTS

Join the crowds at the Sunday morning market in the lovely old town of Teguise (▷ 34–35).
Learn all about lace in the village of Lajares in northern Fuerteventura (▷ 97).
Browse unique pieces of artisan-made jewellery, weaving and ceramics at Fuerteventura's Molino de Antigua (▷ 96).

Teguise Sunday market (above)

FABULOUS FOODS

Pair wonderful wine with imaginative fare at Lilium (▷ 83), Lanzarote's best wine bar.
Bite into a mouthwatering steak at Mesón de la Frontera in Haría (▷ 45).
Indulge in gourmet cuisine at Agua Viva (▷ 81), a gorgeous fine-dining experience.
Treat a loved one to a romantic evening at Caserío de Mozaga (▷ 82).
Try the best in Canarian cooking with a gourmet twist at La Tegala (▷ panel, 84).

Canarian food (above); an aperitif on the shore (below)

SUNDOWNERS BY THE SEA

Sip Cosmopolitans at Marea (▷ 78), Playa Blanca's coolest beach bar.
Soar above the city at Stars Bar (▷ 79), right at the top of the Arrecife Gran Hotel.
Drink in the views from a west-facing table at the seaside village of El Golfo (▷ panel, 83).

Corralejo beach (below)

WATERSPORTS

Hang ten with the surf dudes of Caleta de Famara (▷ 43).
Get airborne by learning to kitesurf in Corralejo (▷ 104).
Carve up the waves on Playa de Sotavento (▷ 93), windsurfing central.

A rustic bar, Pájara (above); bustling nightlife (below)

RUSTIC HIDEAWAYS

Bliss out at Casa Tomarén (▷ 110), bohemian villas with a superb yoga studio.

Get cosy at Casa Isaítas (▷ 109), one of Fuerteventura's loveliest country guesthouses.

PARTYING 'TILL DAWN

Bop to Spanish pop with the locals at Arrecife's dance-bars (▷ 79).

Let your hair down in the late-night bars on Puerto del Carmen's Avenida de las Playas (▷ 79).

Manrique's legacy (below)

FREE ATTRACTIONS

Get into vulcanology at the Centro de Visitantes, Mancha Blanca (▷ 53) then walk the Ruta de Tremesana (▷ 72).

Take in Manrique's monument and museum to traditional pastoralism at the Casa-Museo del Campesino (▷ 55).

Take a dip in the Atlantic from Playa Grande (▷ 62–63) or Playa del Mattoral (▷ 93).

Gran Meliá Salinas hotel (below)

INDULGENT HOTELS

Enjoy the luxury of space at the Hesperia Lanzarote, Puerto Calero (▷ 112).

Discover the fabulous tropical garden at the Gran Meliá Salinas, Costa Teguise (▷ 112).

Relax by a beautiful pool at the Los Jameos Playa, Puerto del Carmen (▷ 112).

Book a seafront villa at the immaculate Heredad Kamezí, Playa Blanca (▷ panel, 112).

ESSENTIAL LANZAROTE AND FUERTEVENTURA **IF YOU LIKE...**

HAVING FUN WITH THE KIDS

Make a splash at Baku (▷ 91), Corralejo's colourful water park.

Ride a camel up a volcano in the Parque Nacional de Timanfaya (▷ 58–59).

Laugh at the crazy sealions at Oasis Park, La Lajita (▷ 99).

UNIQUE HOUSES AND GARDENS

Oasis de los Camellos, La Lajita (above)

Get your fix of modern art and inspirational architecture at the Fundacíon César Manrique (▷ 26–27).

Wander around the beautiful sunken garden of the Jameos del Agua (▷ 28–29).

Admire the splendid cacti at Lanzarote's Jardín de Cactus, Guatiza (▷ 30–31) and Fuerteventura's Jardín Botánico at Oasis Park, La Lajita (▷ 99).

*Manrique sculpture (above)
Parc Nacional de Timanfaya (below)*

VOLCANOES

Hot foot it to Timanfaya (▷ 58–59), to admire the most spectacular lava landscapes in the Canaries.

Visit the Casa de los Volcanes (▷ 28–29) for a mine of information on seismic research.

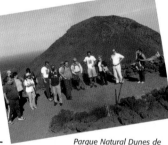

Parque Natural Dunes de Corralejo (below)

TANNING YOUR WHITE BITS

Bare all at Charco del Palo (▷ 36), Lanzarote's east coast nudist colony.

Slap on the sunscreen at Puerto Muelas, the quiet beach on the east side of Punta del Papagayo (▷ 64).

Stretch out in the secluded sands of the Parque Natural de las Dunas de Corralejo (▷ 94–95).

Lanzarote and Fuerteventura by Area

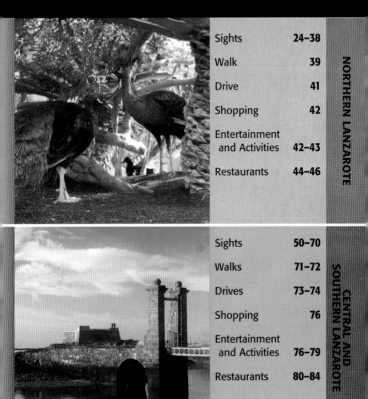

Sights	24–38	
Walk	39	
Drive	41	
Shopping	42	**NORTHERN LANZAROTE**
Entertainment and Activities	42–43	
Restaurants	44–46	

Sights	50–70	
Walks	71–72	
Drives	73–74	**CENTRAL AND SOUTHERN LANZAROTE**
Shopping	76	
Entertainment and Activities	76–79	
Restaurants	80–84	

Sights	88–100	
Drive	101	
Shopping	102	**FUERTEVENTURA**
Entertainment and Activities	102–105	
Restaurants	105–106	

Tour the north for a crash course in the work of Lanzarote's celebrated artist and design guru, César Manrique. Also worth exploring are the graceful old towns of Teguise and Haría, and the stunning coastal wilderness of the Malpaís de la Corona.

Sights	24–38
Walk	39
Drive	41
Shopping	42
Entertainment and Activities	42–43
Restaurants	44–46

Top 25

TOP 25

Cueva de los Verdes ▷ 24
Fundación César Manrique ▷ 26
Jameos del Agua ▷ 28
Jardín de Cactus ▷ 30
La Graciosa ▷ 32
Mirador del Río ▷ 33
Teguise ▷ 34

Northern Lanzarote

ue del
rno

aña Clara

Punta Gorda

Playa
Lambra

152
Montaña
Bermeja

La Graciosa

266
Montaña
Pedro Barba

Punta de Pedro Barba
o de la Sonda

Pedro
Barba

189
ontaña
Mojón

Punta Fariones

Caleta
el Sebo

Caleta del Puerto
de la Sociedad

El Río

Salinas
del Río

Playa de la Cantería

*Bahía
del Salado*
a Francesca

Órzola

Playa del Risco

482
**Mirador
del Río**

Las Tabaibitas

**Caleta del
Mojón Blanco**

Bahía

Ye

213
La
Quamida
de Orzola

Parque
las Pardelas

Casas
la Breña

Punta Prieta

La Caleta

**Guinate
Parque
Tropical**

605
Monte
Corona

Guinate

581

Caleta del
Guincho

Caleta de
las Aulagas

Máguez

Malpaís de Máguez

**Cueva de
los Verdes**

**Jameos
del Agua**

Haría

LZ205

La Negra

Playa la Seba
Punta Mujeres

583
Ganada

LZ10

Caleta del Campo

Chafaris Chafaris

Arrieta

LZ206 **Tabayesco**

Valle del Palomo

Playa de
la Garita

Playa Marina

Punta de la Pared

Mala
Abajo Punta Pasito

Mala

Playa del Seifío

os
alles

**Jardín de
Cactus**

**Charco
del Palo**

LZ405 **Guatiza**

El Mojón 358
Guenia

Urbanización
Los Cocoteros

319
Tinamala

Playa del Tío Joaquín

eseguite

Playa de la Tía Vicenta

Ensenada del Banco

Mulión

Ensenada de
los Barranquillos

229
Cerro Hurón

Urbanización
Cuidad Jardín

Ensenada de
la Gorrina

Playa de los Charcos

Urbanización
osta Teguise

**Costa
Teguise**

Playa
Bastían

Ensenada de las Mármoles

F   **G**   **H**

Cueva de los Verdes

Visitors wait at the cave entrance (right) before venturing inside (left and opposite)

THE BASICS

www.centrosturisticos.com

🔢 G3

✉ LZ–1, Malpaís de la Corona, 28km (17 miles) north of Arrecife

☎ 928 84 84 84

🕐 Daily 10–7

♿ None

💰 Moderate

❓ Guided tours only (50 min; included in admission; last tour 6pm)

HIGHLIGHTS

● Artful lighting and ambient music
● Reflections and optical illusions

TIPS

● The concerts that are occasionally held here aren't widely advertised to tourists: call the centre or check the local press for notices.
● The temperature in the cave is a steady 19ºC (66ºF); you may need an extra layer.

Beneath the ancient lava crust of the Malpaís de la Corona is a mighty cave system that will have you bending double to creep along its tightest passageways, then craning your neck to admire its loftiest ceilings.

Volcanic origins The part of the cave that's open to the public is just a small section of a 7km (4-mile) lava tube that dates back to the eruption of the Volcán de la Corona, around 3,000 to 5,000 years ago, and also includes the Jameos del Agua (▷ 28–29). As molten lava flowed down to the Atlantic, its top layer cooled and hardened; gases trapped under this crust created the tube.

Subterranean secrets This network of underground tunnels and chambers was once a life-saving refuge: islanders hid here in the 16th and 17th centuries to escape marauding pirates and slave-hunters. In the 1960s the island government commissioned Jesús Soto, one of César Manrique's creative collaborators, to turn it into a visitor attraction by designing a route of bridges, stairs and walkways. Its name has nothing to do with colour—Verde (green) was the surname of a family of herders who used to own it—but nonetheless, once your eyes adjust to the atmospheric lighting, you'll begin to pick out a fascinating variety of colours and textures in the lava walls and ceilings. Guides point out curiosities along the route, including a lump of rock that looks a little like a statue of the Madonna. Deep inside the cave is a chamber that is used for concerts.

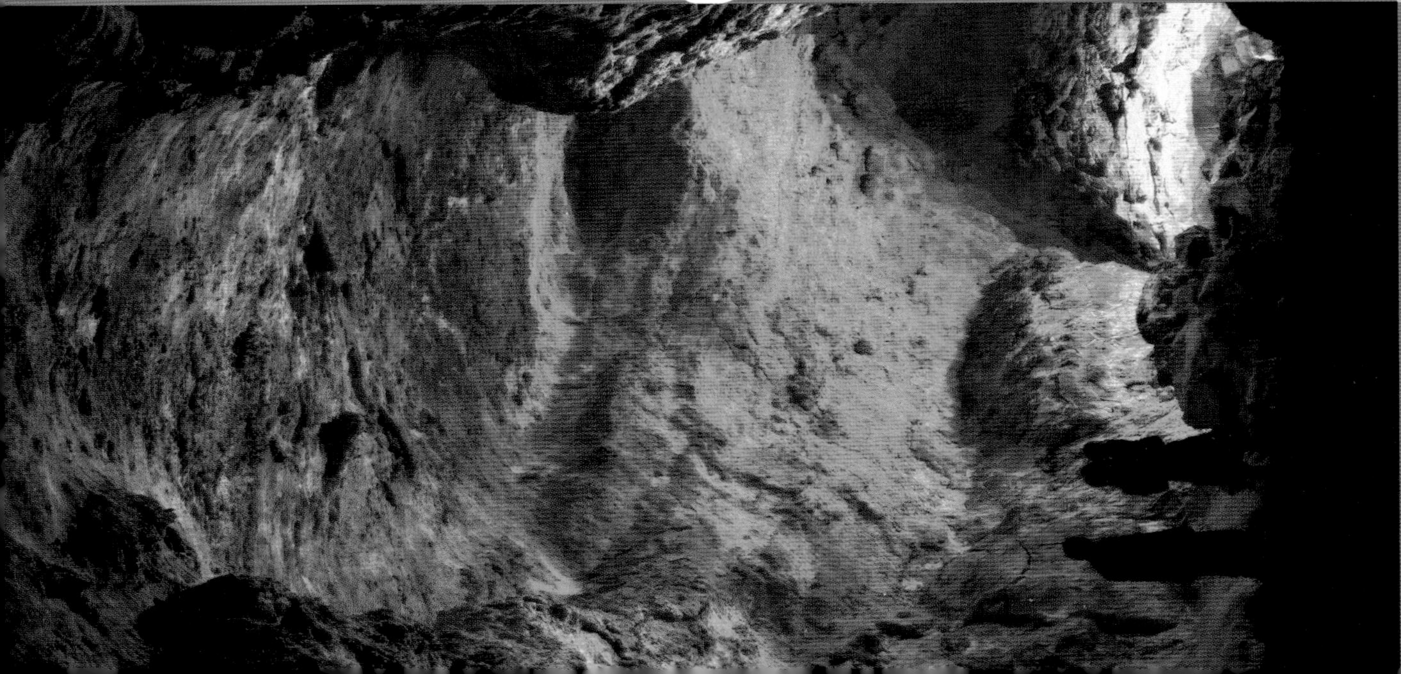

Fundación César Manrique

César Manrique—artist, architect, environmentalist and thinker—was way ahead of his time. His deliciously chic home feels as contemporary today as it did in the 1960s. Now an art museum, it provides a fascinating glimpse into the great man's world.

Unique vision Manrique, who lived from 1919 to 1992, had a colossal influence on the island of his birth: singlehandedly, he sealed Lanzarote's reputation as a destination with real aesthetic and cultural clout. His creative genius gave birth to all the island's most interesting attractions, from the Jameos del Agua (▷ 28–29) to the Jardín de Cactus (▷ 30–31). He was also the driving force behind the conservation principles which, today, the Fundación César Manrique actively promotes.

From the moment you step into the first room and look through the large picture window onto the lunar-like landscape, you begin to appreciate that the entire house and grounds are a testament to Manrique's vision and creativity

Had it not been for his great vision, Lanzarote could have become an overdeveloped mess of high-rise buildings, car parks and billboards.

Home of a genius The Fundación is based in Manrique's former home, which is also an exhibition space for a permanent collection of 20th-century art and temporary displays of new painting, sculpture and photography. The building is fascinating: perched on a lava flow that dates back to the eruptions of the 1730s, its ground floor resembles a traditional Canarian country house, albeit a very light and spacious one, while beneath this are beautiful, cave-like rooms created out of lava bubbles. The whole house celebrates the unique landscape—large windows frame the view and in places, chunks of lava are incorporated into the interior.

THE BASICS

www.fcmanrique.org

🔅 E6

✉ Taro de Tahiche, 5km (3 miles) north of Arrecife

☎ 928 84 31 38

🕐 Jul–end Oct daily 10–7; Nov–end Jun Mon–Sat 10–6, Sun 10–3

🍴 Café

🚌 7, 9, 10, 11, 12, 13

♿ Good

💷 Moderate

Jameos del Agua

TOP 25

- Underground lake
- Sunken gardens and ornamental pool
- La Casa de los Volcanes

TIPS

- The centre's auditorium is closed for renovations; enquire about re-opening.
- Dress up a little if you intend to visit in the evening, when the entrance fee is higher, as the Jameos del Agua attracts a well-groomed crowd.

César Manrique's series of architectural installations got off to an astounding start with this breathtakingly beautiful sunken garden, museum and entertainment venue—an otherworldly space that's quintessentially Lanzarotean.

Water caves Opened in 1966, the Jameos del Agua was a grand showcase for Manrique's creative talents, and, in particular, his interest in embracing and enhancing the natural beauty of Lanzarote's volcanic landscapes. A *jameo* is a sunken, roofless cave in a lava field, formed after the collapse of the roof of a bubble or tube; for his creation, Manrique selected two particularly fine *jameos* in the Malpaís de la Corona, connected by a wide, high-ceilinged tunnel with an underwater lake. A path runs beside the lake,

Clockwise from top left: a volcanic cave; a cave converted into a concert hall; one of the jameos complete with beach and palm trees; looking down onto the restaurant; César Manrique sculpture at the entrance; guests in the rock-hewn restaurant

which is home to a rare species of subterranean crustacean, the *jameito*, which looks a little like a miniature white lobster. The *jameos* themselves are delightful gardens.

Underground chic Visitors to the gardens can relax among lush tropical foliage or beside the perfect ornamental pool, painted in Manrique's trademark glossy white, and shaded by a leaning palm. There's also a vulcanology museum here, La Casa de los Volcanes, with information on the detailed seismic research that's carried out on the island. Lovely by day, the centre is magical after dark—Manrique's guiding vision was to create an unforgettable nightclub. There are two very chic bars, a restaurant serving Canarian cuisine, a performance space for folkloric musicians, and a dance floor.

THE BASICS

www.centrosturisticos.com

➕ G3

✉ LZ-1, Malpaís de la Corona, 28km (17 miles) north of Arrecife

☎ 928 84 80 20

🕐 Mon, Wed, Thu, Sun 10–7, Tue, Fri, Sat 7.30pm–2am

🍴 Restaurant, café and bar

♿ Few

💰 Moderate

Jardín de Cactus

● Well over 7,000 cacti, representing over 1,000 different species

● Restored traditional windmill

TIPS

● The garden is impossible to miss as it's marked by a giant cactus sculpture—one of Manrique's rare creative aberrations.

● The entrance fee includes a drink in the café.

Quirky and fun, César Manrique's fascinating cactus garden reveals his humorous side. To stroll around feels a lot like visiting a sculpture gallery, but with living exhibits.

Beetle farms The quiet little village of Guatiza lies at the heart of Lanzarote's cactus country. Here, farmers have been tending fields of tunera cacti for generations: The plants provide a home for cochineal beetles, whose larvae are harvested and crushed to make cochineal, the main ingredient of natural carmine red dyes. The cochineal industry faded with the invention of artificial dyes, but recent interest in all things organic has brought about a change in fortunes for Lanzarote's cactus farmers, whose product is now in demand once again.

Clockwise from far left: a collection of yellow-green cacti growing in dark volcanic soil; the Jardín de Cactus entrance; details of the different species that grow in the Jardín de Cactus, and in the fields opposite

Cacti as art The Jardín de Cactus is an elegant tribute to this agricultural tradition. It takes the cactus theme and really runs with it, displaying not just Canarian plants but also specimens originating from Africa and the Americas. Manrique sited the garden in a former quarry, lining it with terraced beds to give the space and all the natural drama of an amphitheatre. Columns of rock left behind by the miners add an extra dash of surrealism, as do the individually designed lamps, doorknobs and bins, all inspired by cacti. Visitors can wander up and down the tiers to admire the plants in close up, or climb inside the beautifully restored windmill that sits on top of a small hill at one end. There are also great views from the café. Those who would like to start or embellish their own cactus collection can buy small specimens from the shop.

THE BASICS

www.centrosturisticos.com
🚻 F4
✉ Guatiza, 16km (10 miles) north of Arrecife
☎ 928 52 93 97
🕐 Daily 10–7
🍴 Restaurant and café
🚌 7, 9, 10
♿ Good
💰 Moderate

La Graciosa

An overview of the island, and the cluster of buildings that are confined to one area

THE BASICS

✠ F2

🍴 Restaurants, café/bars

⛴ Órzola to Caleta de Sebo with Líneas Maritímas Romero (tel 902 40 16 66; www.lineas-romero.com), 3–5 crossings each way per day, journey time 20 min, €20 return

HIGHLIGHTS

● Caleta de Sebo
● Playa Francesca
● Playa de las Conchas

TIPS

● The western beaches are not safe for swimming.
● La Graciosa is a traditional Catholic community; it's polite to respect this. Swimming or sunbathing without a bathing suit is frowned upon.
● The island celebrates the Fiesta de Nuestra Señora del Carmen (16 July) in exuberant style with boat parades, music and dancing.

Just a short hop by ferry from Lanzarote, there's a beguiling remoteness and innocence about Isla de la Graciosa, with its simple settlement of fishermen's cottages backed by breezy, unspoilt beaches.

Easternmost island Every day, when the visitors come ashore at Caleta del Sebo's tidy harbour, La Graciosa's tiny population increases by around half. Those who gaze down on the island from the Mirador del Río (▷ 33) may wonder why it is that anyone at all would choose to live in such a barren-looking, isolated spot, but in fact it lies close to some very productive fishing grounds. Today, most of the islanders still make their living from fishing, and you may see fish being sun-dried in the traditional way—sliced open and pegged out on lines.

Caleta de Sebo The village has a couple of rustic harbourside restaurants, a small safe beach and a cluster of whitewashed houses. Walk beyond its fringes and you reach more beaches, entirely undeveloped; the closest is Playa Francesca, while Playa de las Conchas at the foot of Montaña Bermeja on the northwest coast is the most striking.

Protected area La Graciosa is the largest island in the Chinijo archipelago, which is part of a marine reserve that also includes the Risco de Famara coastline. The other islands—Alegranza, Montaña Clara, Roque del Este, Roque del Oeste and some smaller islets—are all uninhabited, with a flourishing population of sea birds.

Mirador del Río

César Manrique's panoramic lookout— poised on the top of the Risco de Famara near Lanzarote's northern tip, with the El Río strait and the Chinijo Archipelago spread below—is a dramatic creation.

Air and water Manrique's sign for the Mirador, a graphic sculpture of a bird and a fish, hints at his theme: the sky and the sea. The building seems unremarkable as you approach; built out of stone that blends with the surroundings, it gives little away, blocking the view it later reveals so splendidly. Inside, there's a moment or two of suspense as you make your way along a curvy white corridor, decorated with rustic ceramics. You then emerge into the main room, a light-drenched space with huge plate glass windows looking out over La Graciosa and beyond.

Drink in the views Sleekly stylish, the room has a bar and a unique ceiling sculpture designed by Manrique to soften the acoustics. Stairs and doorways lead to several open-air viewing terraces, the main one shaped like the prow of a ship and rimmed with a nautical-looking handrail, making you feel you're on an ocean liner ploughing across the Atlantic. Some grumble at the concept of being charged an entrance fee for what they regard as a bar with a view: if it's only the view that interests you, it's worth exploring other points on the coast where you can enjoy it for free. But for anyone interested in the inspirational architectural projects of César Manrique, the Mirador is well worth the small price of admission.

THE BASICS

www.centrosturisticos.com

✚ F2
✉ 37km (23 miles) north of Arrecife, near Yé
☎ 928 52 65 48
🕐 Daily 10–7
🍴 Café-bar (€–€€)
♿ Good
💷 Inexpensive

HIGHLIGHTS

● Viewing terraces at several levels
● Café-bar with an impressive ceiling sculpture

TIP

● The entrance fee includes a drink in the café-bar.

Teguise

HIGHLIGHTS

● Iglesia de Nuestra Señora de Guadeloupe
● Casa-Museo Palacio Spínola
● Centro de Arte Santo Domingo
● *Mercadillo* (Sunday mornings)

TIP

● At the market, skip the stalls selling shoddy souvenirs and head straight for Plaza Clavijo y Fajardo, where the most interesting craft stalls are usually found.
● Climb to the top of Montaña de Guanapay (▷ 36) for great views of the town.

Arguably the most beautiful of Lanzarote's inland towns, Teguise is also the island's oldest. Its Sunday market is fun, but it's also worth visiting on a weekday to appreciate the town's true character.

Conquistadors' capital Founded in the early 1400s, Teguise grew into a small but very prosperous town. On the pleasant square at its heart, Plaza de la Constitución, is a fine church, Nuestra Señora de Guadeloupe, with a lofty bell tower. The plaza is the focus of the action during the *mercadillo* (market), a weekly jamboree where tourists jostle around stalls selling everything from tacky T-shirts to beautiful handmade jewellery, musicians play *timples* (Canarian mandolins) or pan pipes, and traditional wrestlers show off their skills in bouts of *lucha canaria*.

Clockwise from far left: dominating the main square, Iglesia de Nuestra Señora de Guadalupe; inside Convento de Santo Domingo; a view over the town; traditional folk singers entertain at the Sunday market; busy market stalls line the streets on Sunday

Graceful architecture On other days, Teguise is supremely peaceful. There are plenty of colonial buildings to admire, though most keep their charms hidden; it's well worth looking around the Galería La Villa (▷ 42) or the Palacio del Marqués (▷ panel, 45) to see the pretty, flower-filled patios behind the rather inscrutable façades. One grand mansion, the Palacio Spínola on the main church square, is a stately home museum.

Art, food and wine Teguise has an appealingly civilized, arty atmosphere with several excellent, relaxed restaurants and bodegas. Exhibitions of contemporary art, often quite avant-garde, are held in the former church of Santo Domingo on the south side of town, while the numerous attractive gallery shops dotted around provide a hour or two of enjoyable browsing.

THE BASICS

➕ E5
✉ 13km (8 miles) north of Arrecife
🍴 Restaurants, cafés, bars
🚌 7, 9, 10, 11, 12, 13
ℹ Avda Islas Canarias, Centro Comercial Los Charcos, tel 928 82 71 30

Casa-Museo Palacio Spínola
✉ Place de la Constitución
☎ 928 84 51 81
🕐 Mon–Fri and Sun 9–3
♿ Good 💲 Inexpensive

Centro de Arte Santo Domingo
✉ Place General Franco
☎ 928 84 50 01
🕐 Mon–Fri and Sun 10–3
♿ Good 💲 Free

More to See

ARRIETA

This rather plain little coastal town, marked by a large red Manrique wind mobile, has a few fish restaurants and an untouristy feel. The road from here to Órzola is very scenic, with the glittering Atlantic on one side and, on the other, the rugged Malpaís de la Corona, tufted with hardy vegetation.

✚ G4 ✉ 23km (14 miles) north of Arrecife 🍴 Restaurants and cafés in town 🚌 7, 9

CALETA DEL MOJÓN BLANCO

This little-known but highly pictur-esque cove, which is reached via the Arrieta–Órzola road, has safe, shallow water and gleaming white sand scat-tered with volcanic rock pools.

✚ G3 ✉ 34km (21 miles) north of Arrecife 🚌 9

CASTILLO DE SANTA BÁRBARA

Standing guard over Teguise from Montaña de Guanapay, this 16th-century fortress was once used by the desperate citizens as a refuge and defence from bloodthirsty pirates. It now houses an ethnological museum charting the history of the Canarians who emigrated to Cuba and the Americas. It's a steep climb up to the *castillo*, but you can drive to the top.

✚ E5 ✉ 1km (0.6 miles) east of Teguise

Museo del Emigrante Canario

☎ 928 84 50 01 🕐 Jun–end Sep Mon–Fri 10–3, Sun 10–2; Oct–end May Mon–Fri 10–5, Sat–Sun 10–4 🍴 Restaurants and café-bars in Teguise 🚌 7, 9, 10, 11, 12, 13 ♿ Good 👍 Inexpensive

CHARCO DEL PALO

www.charco-del-palo.com

In a secluded part of the northeast coast is this quiet resort, a favourite among German and Scandinavian nudists, many of whom holiday here year after year; the whole village, its beaches and seawater pool are effec-tively clothing-optional.

✚ G4 ✉ 22km (14 miles) north of Arrecife 🍴 Restaurants and café-bars

COSTA TEGUISE

Costa Teguise started out, in the 1970s, as an exclusive resort—César

Fish restaurant by the harbour, Arrieta

Looking toward Órzola, La Caleta

Manrique had a hand in the design of its luxury hotel (the Gran Meliá Salinas; ▷ 112) and the Pueblo Marinero, an authentic-looking recreation of a fishing village complete with whitewashed houses, old-fashioned street lanterns and a bandstand. On Friday evenings, a bazaar-like *mercadillo* selling leather goods, jewellery and oddments takes over the main square. The town has since grown into a brash resort for budget and middle-market tourists, who pack out the bars and the main beach, Playa de las Cucharas. The waters here are both windy and safe, making it a perfect spot for windsurfing lessons; part of the bay is sectioned off for this purpose. Playa de las Cucharas is connected to a string of smaller beaches by a pleasant seafront promenade. On the edge of town are a golf course (▷ 43), a rather dated waterpark, and a brand new aquarium with over 30 tanks displaying Canarian and tropical marine wildlife.

➕ F6 ✉ 7km (4 miles) east of Arrecife 🍴 Restaurants, cafés and bars 🚌 1

Aquapark

✉ Avda Golf 315 ☎ 928 59 21 28 🕐 Daily 10–6 ♿ Good 💶 Expensive

Lanzarote Aquarium

www.aquariumlanzarote.com

✉ CC El Trébol, Avda de las Acacias ☎ 928 59 00 69 🕐 Apr–end Oct 10–7; Nov–end Mar 10–6 ♿ Good 💶 Expensive

GUINATE PARQUE TROPICAL

www.guinatepark.com

Relatively little visited, as it's located in the far north of Lanzarote, this small zoo is home to over 300 captive bird species, including parrots, flamingoes and a gaggle of penguins, plus a few furry creatures such as lemurs and wallabies.

➕ F3 ✉ 35km (22 miles) north of Arrecife ☎ 928 83 55 00 🕐 Daily 10–5 🍴 Restaurant/café ♿ Good 💶 Expensive

HARÍA

Spread gracefully over a well-watered, palm-shaded valley, this sleepy little town of narrow streets and whitewashed houses has a dignified, traditional atmosphere—so much

A colourful bird perched on a tree at Guinate Parque Tropical

Relaxing by the pool at the Gran Meliá Salinas hotel, Costa Teguise

so that César Manrique chose to live here in his old age. There's an artisans' cooperative in the middle of town, where you can see good examples of locally-made lace and basketwork, and on Saturdays, an enjoyable craft and produce market takes place on the central Plaza de Haría.

🔢 F4 ✉ 30km (18 miles) north of Arrecife 🍴 Restaurants, cafés and bars 🚌 7

ÓRZOLA

The main reason to visit the quiet northern fishing village of Órzola is to take the ferry across to La Graciosa (▷ 32), but there's also a row of decent fish restaurants lining the wharf. Just outside town is Las Pardelas, a farm with a collection of domestic animals, which is popular with kids: they can feed vegetables to the goats and rabbits, and ride on the donkeys.

🔢 G2 ✉ 36km (22 miles) north of Arrecife 🍴 Restaurants and café-bars 🚌 9
🚢 Órzola to Caleta de Sebo with Líneas Maritímas Romero (tel 902 40 16 66; www.lineas-romero.com; 3–5 crossings each way per day; journey time 20 min; €20 return)

Parque Las Pardelas
✉ 1km (0.6 mile) south of Órzola 🕾 928 84 25 45 🕔 Daily 10–6 🍴 Restaurant 🚹 Good 💷 Inexpensive

PLAYA DE FAMARA

Famara is considered by connoisseurs to be Lanzarote's most beautiful beach, not only for the stunning backdrop of the sheer Risco de Famara cliffs, but also for its changing light, which is often spectacular at sunset, and its views of the Chinijo archipelago. High winds mean it's not the best place to relax, but it's a mecca for surfers and kitesurfers, many of whom you'll find hanging out in the low-key, sandy village of Caleta de Famara. Although there are no hotels in town, there are plenty of villas and apartments to rent: the kitesurf schools can usually recommend places.

🔢 E4 ✉ 26km (16 miles) north of Arrecife 🍴 Restaurants and café-bars in Caleta de Famara 🚌 20

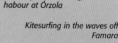

A fishing boat entering the habour at Órzola

Kitesurfing in the waves off Famara

A Walk Around La Graciosa

This walk takes you around the northernmost inhabited island in the Canaries, striding along sandy tracks through desert landscapes.

DISTANCE: 18km (11 miles)   **ALLOW:** 4 hours

START

CALETA DEL SEBO
🚩 F2

1 From the harbour at Caleta del Sebo (▷ 32), walk along the quayside to the village beach, Playa La Laja, then turn inland along Calle La Popa. At the edge of the village, continue north along the dirt road.

2 This road leads toward the centre of the island, with Montaña del Mojón on the left and Las Agujas to the right. In the distance, you can see Isla de Montaña Clara.

3 At a fork in the track, turn right, heading toward Pedro Barba, a cluster of holiday homes forming a coastal hamlet.

4 At the next fork, instead of following the track that leads down to the hamlet, turn left to continue north around the northern slopes of the Pedro Barba ridge.

END

CALETA DEL SEBO

8 This track runs between the two volcanoes and takes you back to Caleta del Sebo.

7 To the south you can see the Risco de Famara, Lanzarote's dramatic northern cliffs. Beyond Las Conchas, turn left to follow the main track south toward Montaña del Mojón and Las Agujas del Sebo.

6 Walk toward the foot of Montaña Bermeja, then turn left to follow the track southwest, in the direction of Caleta del Sebo and Lanzarote. To your right is Playa de las Conchas, the island's most striking beach.

5 From here, there are views of the rocky island of Alegranza.

A Drive Around Northern Lanzarote

Twisting mountain roads offer scenic drama and along the way are some prime examples of Manrique's creative genius.

DISTANCE: 61km (38 miles)　　**ALLOW:** 4–8 hours

START

FUNDACIÓN CÉSAR MANRIQUE
✚ E6

1 Start your trip by marvelling at Manrique's former home (▷ 26–27). When you're ready to move on, turn left at the roundabout marked by the artist's striking 'whisk' wind mobile.

2 Take the LZ-10 to Tahiche and Teguise. The historic town of Teguise (▷ 34–35) is well worth a wander, and it also makes an excellent stop for lunch.

3 As you leave, you could make a detour up the Montaña de Guanapay to admire the view from the Castillo de Santa Bárbara (▷ 36).

4 Heading north, the LZ-10 climbs onto a plateau dotted with wind turbines, then winds its way down via some thrilling hairpin bends, with viewpoints along the way.

END

FUNDACIÓN CÉSAR MANRIQUE

8 To drop in at the Jardín del Cactus (▷ 30–31), turn off at Mala or Guatiza. To complete the loop, follow the LZ-1 south toward Arrecife.

7 About 8km (5 miles) southeast of the Mirador, turn left toward the sea for the Cueva de los Verdes (▷ 24) and Jameos del Agua (▷ 28–29). Take the LZ-1 south, following the coast past Punta Mujeres and Arrieta (▷ 36).

6 Continue north to Yé then turn left to the Mirador del Río (▷ 33), a beautiful spot for a drink and a stroll. Rejoin the main road as it skirts around Monte Corona.

5 Around 17km (10.5 miles) north of Teguise, you reach the small town of Haría (▷ 37–38), nestled in a valley.

Shopping

ARTESANÍA LANZAROTE

At this shop in old Teguise items on sale include traditional hats, embroidered tablecloths, jewellery, timples (small 4 or 5-stringed Canarian guitars) and local food products.

➕ F5 ✉ Pl Constitución 12, Teguise ☎ 928 84 51 06 🚌 7, 9, 10, 11, 12, 13

ATELIER ARTE & CERÁMICA

Attractive and welcoming studio-gallery run by a painter and a ceramicist, both from Germany, as a showcase for their work.

➕ F5 ✉ Avda Acorán 43–45, Teguise ☎ 928 84 56 50 🚌 7, 9

CASA DE LA PALMERA

Craft and gift shop, good for locally-made products such as aloe vera, jars of *mojo*, Canarian honey, cactus jam from Guatiza and Malvasía wine from La Geria.

➕ F5 ✉ Pl Constitución, Teguise 🚌 7, 9, 10, 11, 12, 13

LA LONJA FUNDACIÓN CÉSAR MANRIQUE

Quality T-shirts, tiles,

MERCADILLOS

By far the most famous of the island's weekly craft and souvenir markets is the *mercadillo,* which swamps Teguise every Sunday from around 10am until 2pm (▷ 34–35). Tiny by comparison, but with a more authentic village feel, is Haría's *mercadillo* (▷ 38), held on Saturdays (10–2). On Fridays from 6pm, an evening *mercadillo* with a fun atmosphere takes over Costa Teguise's Pueblo Marinero (▷ 37).

---

bags, prints and other souvenirs featuring Manrique's distinctive graphics, plus art books. There's another branch at the airport.

➕ E5 ✉ Taro de Tahiche, Teguise 🚌 7, 9, 10, 11, 12, 13

MAGMA ART

Tiny jewellery boutique with an attractive collection of artisan-made pieces featuring amber, olivina and lava beads set in silver.

➕ E5 ✉ C/ José Antonio, Teguise 🚌 7, 9, 10, 11, 12, 13

TIERRA

A wonderful little emporium stuffed with earthy ceramics, clothing, pictures and oddments inspired by local wildlife and ancient Canarian symbology.

➕ E5 ✉ C/ Higuera, Teguise ☎ 928 84 57 01 🚌 7, 9, 10, 11, 12, 13

Entertainment and Activities

CALIMA SURF

www.calimasurf.com Calima Surf offers good-quality instruction in surfing and kitesurfing, catering for all levels from beginners up.

➕ E4 ✉ C/ Achique 14, La Caleta Famara ☎ 928 52 85 28 🚌 20

CALIPSO DIVING

www.calipso-diving.com Reliable operator covering the coast from Charco del Palo to Costa Teguise, and offering PADI training courses.

➕ F6 ✉ Avda Islas Canarias, Costa Teguise ☎ 928 59 08 79 🚌 1

CLUB BUCEO PUNTA FARIONES

www.buceolanzarote.com Specializes in trips to challenging diving sites found around the north coast and La Graciosa.

➕ G2 ✉ Restaurante Punta Fariones, Órzola ☎ 928 84 25 58 or 696 90 06 52 🚌 9

CLUB NATHALIE SIMON

www.sportaway-lanzarote.com
Highly respected wind-surfing training centre running classes on Playa de las Cucharas.
➕ F6 ✉ C/ Olas, Costa Teguise ☎ 928 59 07 31 🚌 1

COSTA N-OESTE

www.costanoroeste.com
This is Lanzarote's best known surfing and kitesurfing outfit. Runs week-long Surf Camps for beginners, with accommodation in Famara or La Santa. Also offers advanced tuition.
➕ E4 ✉ C/ Marinero, La Caleta de Famara ☎ 928 52 85 97 or 620 95 60 64 🚌 20

FAMARA SURF

www.famarasurf.com
Surf shop offering gear and tuition; the staff can also fix up local accommodation.
➕ E4 ✉ Avda El Marinero 39, La Caleta de Famara ☎ 928 52 86 76 or 696 24 19 52 🚌 20

GOLF COSTA TEGUISE

www.lanzarote-golf.com
This, Lanzarote's original 18-hole golf course, is surprisingly leafy and green, with well-tended gardens that are home to hoopoes and other wild birds. The club house has a pleasant veranda with fine views of the course, and is a good spot for lunch or a drink.
➕ F6 ✉ Avda del Golf, Costa Teguise ☎ 928 59 05 12 🚌 1

HOTSTICK

www.kiteschoolspain.com
This kitesurfing school is based in Costa Teguise but operates in Famara. They use walkie-talkie equipment for in situ tuition.
➕ F6 ✉ CC Puerto Tahiche 6, Paseo Marítimo, Costa Teguise ☎ 928 82 61 00 or 647 15 55 16 🚌 1

JAMEOS DEL AGUA

www.centrosturisticos.com
César Manrique's chic sunken garden takes on a glittering atmosphere after dark, when there's live music and after-dinner dancing.
➕ G3 ✉ LZ-1 road, Malpaís de la Corona ☎ 928 84 80 20 🕐 Tue, Fri and Sat 7pm–2am

---

RIDE THE WAVES

Northern Lanzarote's windsurfing and surfing seasons dovetail neatly. The best winds for windsurfing and kitesurfing blow from late March to September or October, with sailboard championships taking place in Costa Teguise in June and July. In the winter months, hardcore surfers head straight for Famara and La Santa (▷ 70) in the rugged northwest of the island, to catch the best waves as they come rolling in.

LAGOMAR

www.lag-o-mar.com
In the striking volcanic cliffside garden of a house originally designed by César Manrique for Omar Sharif, this very stylish, semi-outdoor venue combines a fine-dining restaurant and a classy dance bar. Live jazz on Sundays from 2–4.
➕ E5 ✉ C/ Loros 6, Nazaret ☎ 928 84 56 65 🕐 Tue–Sat 12–12, Sun 12–6 🚌 7, 9, 10

LÍNEAS MARÍTIMAS ROMERO

www.lineas-romero.com
As well as running a ferry service between Órzola and Caleta del Sebo (▷ 38), this boat company runs leisurely cruises around the Chinijo archipelago, stopping at La Graciosa's Playa Francesca for a refreshing swim.
➕ F2 ✉ C/ García Escámez 11, Caleta del Sebo, La Graciosa ☎ 928 84 20 55 🚌 9

PUEBLO MARINERO

Yet another César Manrique creation, this village-style square started life, back in the 1970s, as an exclusive hangout but is now packed out with rather raucous pubs and cocktail bars; Chispas and Hook are among the most popular places to hangout.
➕ F6 ✉ Avda Islas Canarias, Costa Teguise 🕐 Daily 10am–late, cocktail bars from 7pm 🚌 1

Restaurants

PRICES

Prices are approximate, based on a 3-course meal for one person.
€€€ over €32
€€ €20–€32
€ under €20

ACATIFE (€€)

Acatife (the old name for Teguise) is housed in an atmospheric mansion, and claims to be Lanzarote's oldest restaurant. Traditional food is served such as roasted kid or rabbit in red wine, and a there is a polite, conservative atmosphere.
🚹 E5 ☒ C/ San Miguel 4, Teguise ☎ 928 84 50 37 🕔 Daily lunch, dinner 🚌 7, 9, 10, 11, 12, 13

AMANECER (€€)

The locals' favourite for fresh fish and seafood, this long-established spot packs out at weekends. The terrace at the back overlooks the bay.
🚹 G4 ☒ C/ Garita 46, Arrieta ☎ 928 84 82 66 🕔 Mon–Wed, Fri–Sun 12–8 🚌 7, 9

LA BODEGUITA DEL MEDIO (€)

This convivial little bar serves tasty plates of tapas at low prices, and is always buzzing on Sundays when the market's in full swing.
🚹 E5 ☒ Pl Clavijo y Fajardo, Teguise ☎ 928 84 56 80 🕔 Mon–Fri lunch, dinner, Sat–Sun lunch only 🚌 7, 9, 10, 11, 12, 13

LAS BRASAS (€€)

In a district that's always packed with holidaymakers, this is a determinedly untouristy little restaurant, serving straightforward fare such as steak and chops.
🚹 F6 ☒ Pl Pueblo Marinero 3, Costa Teguise ☎ 928 59 07 61 🕔 Tue–Sun dinner only 🚌 1

CAFÉ JALEO (€)

One of the few places on Lanzarote that takes particular pride in its vegetarian dishes, such as lentil curry or goat's cheese quiche. This large café has an arty, community centre feel, with regular exhibitions and live music.
🚹 E5 ☒ Casa Santiago, C/ Flores, Teguise ☎ 928 84 56 63 🕔 Sun–Fri 10–5 🚌 7, 9, 10, 11, 12, 13

COUNTRY COOKING

For the best in Lanzarotean cuisine, it pays to be a little adventurous, and go where the locals go: inland, where rustic village restaurants serve up imaginative tapas, hearty roasts and delicious stews. There's no need to feel intimidated, even the most offbeat places are very welcoming to visitors and most have menus with English (and German) translations—just ask.

CASA GARCÍA (€€)

This unsophisticated but very popular village restaurant serves up simple local fish dishes, grills and freshly made pizzas in a large, bright and airy dining room.
🚹 E4 ☒ Avda Marinero 1, La Caleta de Famara ☎ 928 52 87 10 🕔 Tue–Sun lunch, dinner 🚌 20

CHARCO VIEJO (€€)

A friendly harbourside fish and shellfish restaurant with an open kitchen where you can watch the cooks at work. Try the catch of the day. The mixed fish grill is another favourite.
🚹 G2 ☒ C/ La Quemadita, Órzola ☎ 928 84 25 91 🕔 Daily lunch, dinner 🚌 9

EL CHARCÓN (€€)

www.elcharcon.com
You can't get much closer to the sea than this restaurant serving fish, seafood and Canarian dishes, in a pretty fishing village. Choose from tuna, sea bass, sole and sardines, plus a range of meat and salad dishes.
🚹 F4 ☒ Arrieta Harbour, Haría ☎ 928 84 81 10 🕔 Mon–Tue, Thu–Sun lunch, dinner 🚌 9

EL CHIRINGUITO CASA GARCÍA (€)

This is a favourite hangout of chilled-out dudes with sunbleached hair who like to swap surfing stories over a beer and sandwiches.

E4 ⌧ C/ Marinero 16, La Caleta de Famara ☎ No phone ⏰ Tue–Sun lunch, dinner 🚌 20

DOMUS POMPEI (€)

www.domuspompei.com
Friendly, reasonably priced Italian in a quiet part of Costa Teguise near Playa Bastián, with a selection of tasty pizzas and pasta dishes.
F6 ⌧ C/ Taibaba 2, Costa Teguise ☎ 928 82 71 12 ⏰ Daily lunch, dinner 🚌 1

LA GALERÍA (€)

This cosy little bar, a few steps from Teguise's main square, serves good tapas, fish and light meals, and sometimes hosts live music events.
E5 ⌧ C/ Nueva 8, Teguise ☎ 928 84 54 28 ⏰ Mon 11.30–4, Tue–Fri 11.30–10, Sat 11.30–4, Sun 11.30–10 🚌 7, 9, 10, 11, 12, 13

LA GRACIOSA (€€€)

Elegant and refined, this fine-dining restaurant is in a league of its own in Costa Teguise. A good choice for a special occasion. Superb fresh lobster, foie gras and prime sirloin regularly appear on the menu.
F6 ⌧ Hotel Gran Meliá Salinas, Avda Islas Canarias, Costa Teguise ☎ 928 59 00 40 ⏰ Daily dinner high season only 🚌 1

LOS HELECHOS (€)

Most people come to this canteen restaurant

for the panoramic views rather than the food, but it's actually great value for a simple, tasty Canarian-style lunch.
F4 ⌧ LZ-10, 5km (3 miles) south of Haría ☎ 928 83 50 89 ⏰ Daily 10–6

IKARUS (€€€)

Self-consciously cool, this town-centre bistro serves imaginative dishes such as spinach and goat's cheese lasagne, or crêpes with apples and calvados.
E5 ⌧ Pl Dieciocho de Julio, Teguise ☎ 928 84 53 32 ⏰ Tue–Sat dinner only 🚌 7, 9, 10, 11, 12, 13

MESÓN DE LA FRONTERA (€€€)

Serving probably the best steak on the island, tucked away on a back-street on the north side

PATIO DEL VINO

The owner of Teguise's old-est mansion, a 15th-century *palacio*, is a wine expert who has turned his gorgeous, flower-filled patio into a place to enjoy good wine. There's no menu; instead the waiter brings you a generous plate of delicious nibbles to accompany your choice.

Palacio Del Marqués
E5 ⌧ C/ Herrera y Rojas 9, Teguise ☎ 928 84 53 73 ⏰ Apr–end Oct Mon–Fri 12–8, Sun 10–3; Nov–end Mar Mon–Fri 12–6, Sun 10–3 🚌 7, 9, 10, 11, 12, 13

of the village of Haría. Mouthwatering cuts are faultlessly prepared by dedicated staff who really know their stuff.
F4 ⌧ C/ Casa Atrás 4, Haría ☎ 928 83 53 10 ⏰ Mon–Sat 12–9.30, Sun 12–5 🚌 7

MESÓN LA JORDANA (€€)

Always a safe bet, this long-established Mediterranean-style res-taurant is a good place to try local fish or rabbit.
F6 ⌧ CC Lanzarote Bay 10-11, C/ Geranios, Costa Teguise ☎ 928 59 03 28 ⏰ Mon–Sat lunch, dinner 🚌 1

NEPTUNO (€€)

The best place to eat in the Jablillo area of Costa Teguise, this pleasantly old-fashioned restaurant has good Canarian and international dishes, such as grilled fish with *papas arrugadas* or steak cas-serole, and also a great wine list.
F6 ⌧ CC Neptuno 6, Avda Jablillo, Costa Teguise ☎ 928 59 03 78 ⏰ Mon–Sat lunch only 🚌 1

OSCAR'S (€€)

Attractive, with a relaxed atmosphere and a menu of quality dishes from all over the world—from spicy sesame sea bass to classic surf-and-turf or beef stroganoff—this is highly popular with British holidaymakers.
F6 ⌧ Avda Mar 24, Las

Coronas, Costa Teguise
☎ 928 59 04 89 🕔 Mon–Wed, Fri–Sun dinner only 🚌 1

EL PASTELITO (€)

Great little no-frills bakery-café with delicious cakes and sandwiches, freshly made on the premises, a short drive from the Fundación César Manrique.
➕ F6 ✉ Avda N Torre 22, Tahiche (on the LZ-1 to Jameos del Agua) ☎ 928 84 33 16 🕔 Tue–Sun lunch, dinner 🚌 7, 9, 10

PATIO CANARIO (€€)

If you're new to Canarian tapas, this is a great place to start. Attractive and informal, there's a choice of indoor seating or outdoor tables in a leafy square, and a great menu with helpful photos to guide your choice.
➕ F6 ✉ Plaza Pueblo Marinero, Costa Teguise ☎ 928 34 62 34 🕔 Daily lunch, dinner 🚌 1

PERLA DEL ATLÁNTICO (€€)

A short walk from the main row of restaurants close to Órzola's ferry and fishing port, this place has good views over the water and a long menu of fish and seafood dishes.
➕ G2 ✉ Avda Caletón 3, Órzola ☎ 928 81 11 15 🕔 Daily lunch, dinner 🚌 9

PUNTA FARIONES (€€)

Fish restaurant with a good reputation and an interior decked out in suitably nautical style.
➕ G2 ✉ Paseo Marítimo 10, Órzola ☎ 928 84 25 58 🕔 Daily lunch, dinner 🚌 9

RESTAURANTE SOL (€€)

www.restaurantesolfamara.com
Frequented by locals, this restaurant by the beach serves tasty grilled fish, seafood and Canarian cuisine.
➕ E4 ✉ C/ Salvavidas 48, La Caleta de Famara ☎ 928 52 87 88 🕔 Daily lunch, dinner 🚌 20

EL RISCO (€€)

This spotless family-run restaurant was once owned by relatives of Manrique, whose artwork graces the walls. Good for fish and salads. Large windows look out over the sea and the dramatic Risco de Famara cliffs.
➕ E4 ✉ C/ Montaña

LIGHT BITES

If you're not too hungry, or are feeling a little hard up, tapas can be a good option, as each dish is moderately sized and priced. Beware, though, tapas dishes may be richer than you expect and when presented with a long, tempting menu, it's easy to order more than you can manage. Starters, particularly salads, are often quite large; but it's perfectly acceptable to share.

Clara 30, La Caleta de Famara ☎ 928 52 85 50 🕔 Mon–Wed, Fri–Sun lunch, dinner 🚌 20

LAS TRES LUNAS (€€)

In a quiet coastal town, this friendly little place serves huge plates of good fish on a terrace with sea views.
➕ G4 ✉ C/ Salinas, Punta Mujeres ☎ 928 17 34 16 🕔 Daily lunch, dinner 🚌 9

EL VARADERO (€€)

Pleasant harbourside fish restaurant—the top lunchtime choice of those visiting Isla de la Graciosa for the day.
➕ F2 ✉ Avda Virgen del Mar 125, La Graciosa ☎ 928 84 21 75 🕔 Daily lunch, dinner 🚢 From Órzola (▷ 38)

VESUBIO (€)

Busy pizzeria-grill offering masses of choice, including plenty of main courses for under €10, and views of the coast south of Costa Teguise.
➕ F6 ✉ Playa de Jablillo, Costa Teguise ☎ 928 59 00 90 🕔 Daily lunch, dinner 🚌 1

VILLA TOLEDO (€€)

Reasonably priced eatery with huge oceanfront terraces, set apart from the bustle of central . Costa Teguise.
➕ F6 ✉ Los Cocoderos, Playa Bastián, Costa Teguise ☎ 928 59 06 26 🕔 Daily lunch, dinner 🚌 1

Sunnier than the north, this area is home to the island's two largest resorts, Puerto del Carmen and Playa Blanca, and the island's capital, Arrecife. All are within easy reach of astounding volcanoes, intriguing wine-lands and the delightful Papagayo beaches.

Sights	**50–70**
Walks	**71–72**
Drives	**73–74**
Shopping	**76**
Entertainment and Activities	**76–79**
Restaurants	**81–84**

Top 25
TOP 25

Arrecife ▷ **50**
Castillo de San José ▷ **52**
Centro de Visitantes e Interpretación ▷ **53**
El Golfo ▷ **54**
Monumento al Campesino ▷ **55**
Museo Agrícola El Patio ▷ **56**
Parque Nacional de Timanfaya ▷ **58**
Playa Blanca ▷ **60**
Playa Grande ▷ **62**
Punta de Papagayo ▷ **64**
Yaiza ▷ **65**
Valle de la Geria ▷ **66**

Central and Southern Lanzarote

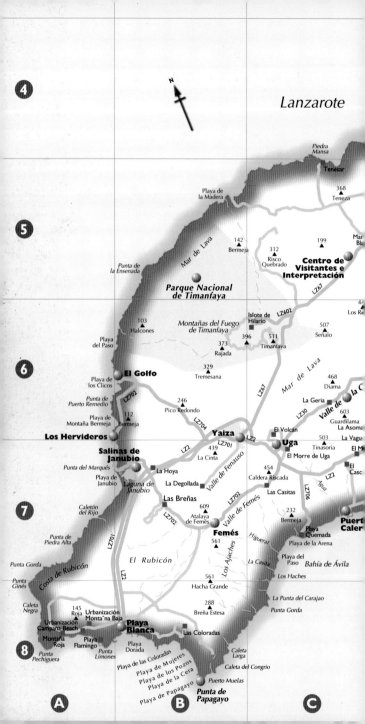

Lanzarote

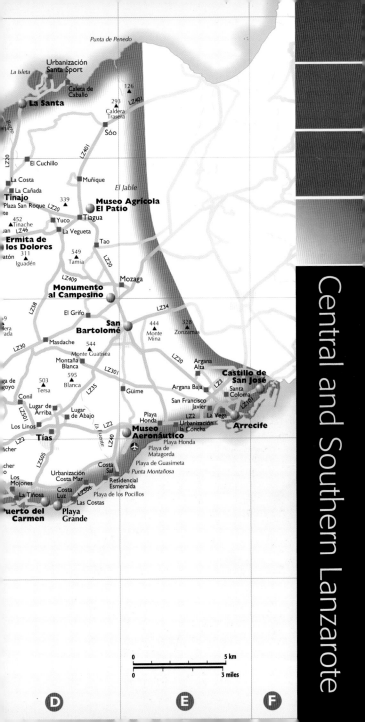

Punta de Penedo

La Isleta
Urbanización
Santa Sport
Caleta de
Caballo
La Santa
126 ▲
LZ401
293 ▲
Caldera
Trasera
Sóo

LZ20
El Cuchillo
LZ401
La Costa
La Cañada
Muñique
El Jable
Tinajo
Plaza San Roque LZ20
te
339 ▲
**Museo Agrícola
El Patio**
452 ▲Tinache
uan LZ46
Yuco
Tiagua
La Vegueta
**Ermita de
los Dolores**
atón
311 ▲
Iguadén
Tao
549 ▲
Tamia

LZ409
Mozaga
**Monumento
al Campesino**

LZ58
El Grifo
LZ34
9
era
ada
**San
Bartolomé**
444 ▲
Monte
Mina
326 ▲
Zonzamas

LZ30
Masdache
544 ▲
Monte Guatisea
LZ20
Argana
Alta
**Castillo de
San José**
Montaña
Blanca
595 ▲
Blanca
LZ301
Argana Baja
Santa
Coloma

ga de
goyo
503 ▲
Tersa
LZ35
Güime
San Francisco
Javier
Arrecife
Conil
Lugar de
Arriba
Lugar
de Abajo
Playa
Honda
LZ2
Urbanización
la Concha
La Vega
LZ2_01

LZ250
Los Linos
Tías
**Museo
Aeronáutico**
Playa Honda
cher
o
LZ505
Costa
Sal
Playa de
Matagorda
Los
Mojones
Urbanización
Costa Mar
Residencial
Esmeralda
Playa de Guasimeta
Punta Montañosa
La Tiñosa
Costa
Luz
LZ506
Las Costas
Playa de los Pocillos
**Puerto del
Carmen**
**Playa
Grande**

0   5 km
0   3 miles

D   E   F

Central and Southern Lanzarote

Arrecife

HIGHLIGHTS

● El Charco de San Ginés
● Castillo de San Gabriel
● Castillo de San José
● Iglesia de San Ginés
● La Recova

TIPS

● Most of Arrecife's shops close from 2–5.
● You can catch a *guagua* (bus) to most parts of the island from Arrecife's bus station.

Sleepy in the afternoons but bustling in the mornings and evenings, Arrecife is a hard-working capital with the atmosphere of a provincial Spanish town. It probably won't rock your world, but it's a pleasant place for a stroll.

Quiet capital Crammed around a sheltered stretch of coast with a peaceful tidal lagoon, Arrecife is a modest city. It took over from Teguise as Lanzarote's capital in 1852, by which time it was a thriving commercial centre with two forts, the 16th-century Castillo de San Gabriel, now a small local history museum, and the 18th-century Castillo de San José (▷ 52). San Gabriel is linked to the town by an unusual bridge, the Puenta de las Bolas (or Cannonball Bridge). A craft market takes place in Arrecife every Wednesday 9–3.

Clockwise from top left: whitewashed houses seen beyond moored fishing boats at El Charco de San Ginés; under an orange sunset, boats are moored in the natural lagoon; the tree-lined courtyard of San Ginés church; two cannons at the front of the Castillo de San Gabriel, built to protect the town from pirate attack

The seafront and lagoon The most attractive area to explore lies between the city's clean and pleasant beach, Playa del Reducto, and the lagoon, El Charco de San Ginés, a harbour for fishing boats. The two are connected by a renovated promenade, Avenida La Marina, lined with tropical gardens and a bandstand. There's also a walkway around the lagoon. The cluster of old streets just south of the lagoon are graced by the parish church of San Ginés and a newly restored marketplace, La Recova, where shops and stalls sell fresh local bread, fruit, cheese and wine. Just west of here is the shopping district, much of which is pedestrianized; its main street, Calle de León y Castillo, is a pleasantly low-key jumble of surf-gear outlets and old-fashioned outfitters. Café tables spill out onto the pavements of the side streets nearby.

THE BASICS

🔒 E6

🍴 Restaurants, cafés and bars

🚌 1, 2, 5, 6, 7, 9, 10, 14, 16, 19, 20, 21, 22, 23, 24, 26

🚢 Direct service to Tenerife, Gran Canaria, La Palma, El Hierro and Madeira with Naviera Armas (www.naviera-armas.com)

ℹ️ C/ Blas Cabrera Felipe, tel 928 81 17 62

Castillo de San José

TOP 25

The fort set in a sculpture garden (left) and its restaurant overlooking the water (right)

THE BASICS

www.centrosturisticos.com

✚ F6

✉ Arrecife

☎ 928 81 23 21

🕐 MIAC daily 11–9

🍴 Restaurant and bar

🚌 1

♿ Good

💷 Inexpensive

HIGHLIGHTS

● Works by Tàpies, Millares and Sempere

● Stylish and upmarket restaurant and bar

TIP

● If you'd just like to visit the restaurant or bar without viewing the art, you're not required to pay the admission fee: use the entrance on the lower level.

Arrecife's 18th-century fort was an unremarkable building—low, blank-fronted and plain—until César Manrique's magic touch transformed it from unloved hulk to compelling art statement.

International art Now, the Castillo is surrounded by a sculpture garden of groomed volcanic gravel, and the main part of the interior is a 20th-century art museum, the Museo Internacional de Arte Contemporáneo (MIAC). When it opened in 1976, MIAC was the island's first international cultural institution. On the lower level, Manrique created a restaurant, with huge ocean-facing windows and a timelessly stylish 1970s look.

Spanish abstracts Built in the 1770s and completed in 1779, the fort has a very simple, two-floor layout. Constructed of solid basalt blocks, the project provided much-needed work for the poverty-stricken islanders who had yet to recover from the catastrophic volcanic eruptions of the 1730s. The barrel-vaulted upper floor, entered via a drawbridge, is used as an exhibition space for the permanent collection, which includes Spanish abstract art from the 1950s, 60s and 70s by Tàpies, Millares and Sempere, as well as eruption-inspired paintings by Manrique himself. Paved with dark slabs and pebbles, and walled with rock, the space has a brooding rawness that makes a striking backdrop for the paintings and sculptures. Pick up an English language audio guide for background information on the exhibits. A curvy staircase leads down to an exhibition space and the restaurant.

The visitor centre traces the creation of the island's volcanic landscape

Centro de Visitantes e Interpretación

Watch documentaries about Lanzarote's fiery history, then feel the earth move in a simulation chamber that gives a scaled-down impression of the roar and rumble of Timanfaya in spate.

Earth-shattering events The volcanic eruptions that shook Lanzarote from 1730 to 1736 and again in 1824 transformed the natural environment and had a profound effect on Lanzarote's cultural and financial fortunes. The Centro de Interpretación, which lies on the northeastern edge of the Parque Natural de los Volcanes and the Parque Nacional de Timanfaya, provides background information on the cataclysmic changes that took place. Although many visitors approach Timanfaya from the southwest side of the park, it's well worth visiting this centre before you tour the Ruta de los Volcanes, as it will enhance your appreciation of the landscape.

Turbulent years Relatively little documentation relating to the circumstances of the eruptions survives but research has pieced together an informative picture. Particularly striking are the displays showing the sequence in which the volcanoes exploded and scale models of the island and the archipelago that reveal their precise alignment. Much of the exhibition is on present-day ecology, with descriptions of the rare lizards, birds and lichens that eke out a living in the lava fields. The volcanoes now appear to be cooling with no further eruptions imminent. Outside there is a platform from which you can survey the eerie scene.

THE BASICS

➕ C5

✉ Crta Yaiza-Tinajo, 25km (16 miles) northwest of Arrecife, near Mancha Blanca

☎ 928 84 08 39

🕐 Daily 9–5

♿ Good

🎟 Free

❓ Audiovisual documentaries are shown on the half hour

HIGHLIGHTS

● Eruption simulator
● Viewing platform overlooking the *malpaís* (badlands)

TIPS

● Bring your own headphones to hear the audiovisual voiceover in English.
● The centre is the starting point for the Ruta de Tremesana (▷ 72).

El Golfo

Boats rest on the black sands (left); a lagoon lies in the rim of a volcanic crater (right)

THE BASICS

🗺 B6
✉ 32km (20 miles) west of Arrecife
🍴 Restaurants and café-bars

HIGHLIGHTS

● Lago de los Clicos
● Rustic fish restaurants

Created by the explosive collision of boiling lava and Atlantic waves, the El Golfo crater has inspired numerous artists and photographers, most recently the famous Spanish film-maker Pedro Almodóvar.

Oceanfront crater El Golfo lies at the western limit of a string of volcanic cones that stretches right across the Parque Nacional de Timanfaya. Most of these didn't exist prior to the eruptions of the 1770s, when the coastline was entirely remodelled by fresh lava. El Golfo is the crater of an extinct volcano whose oceanward side has collapsed, leaving a semi-circular amphitheatre of rock with an unusual, semi-molten appearance, streaked with a vivid combination of shades from black to deep russet. Particularly striking is the green lagoon at the rear of the crater, El Lago (or El Charco) de los Clicos, separated from the ocean by a black beach, the Playa de los Clicos, but connected to it by underground volcanic tubes. You're not allowed to walk up to the rim of the lagoon but you can admire it from a distance; the best view is from the elevated walkway accessed from the village of El Golfo.

Famous for fish Just north of the crater, perched between the ocean and Timanfaya's vast sea of lava, is the small fishing village of El Golfo. It's an isolated place best-known for its fish restaurants (▷ panel, 83): sitting side by side on the seafront, with tables overlooking the black, stony beach. Like Famara (▷ 38), this is a good spot from which to watch the sun setting over the sea.

Manrique's white Monumento al Campesino, located at the centre of the island

Monumento al Campesino

This striking Cubist sculpture by César Manrique, honours Lanzarote's peasant farmers. Towering over the Casa-Museo del Campesino and floodlit by night, it can be seen from quite a distance.

Fertility monument Manrique had a great respect for the peasant farmers (*campesinos*) who managed to turn Lanzarote's harsh, arid environment into fertile farmland, through ingenuity and hard graft. In this sculpture, symbolically located in the geographical centre of the island, he paid tribute to their efforts, and to the island's hardy fishermen. The work, whose alternative title is Monumento a la Fecundidad (Monument to Fertility), is an abstract representation of a peasant with three domestic animals around him. Assembled from objects such as the water-tanks from boats, positioned on a natural mound and painted white, it was completed in 1968.

Museum of rural culture The Casa-Museo del Campesino, also designed by Manrique, is a recreation of a traditional homestead complete with whitewashed walls, turretted chimneys, green-painted timbers and an airy central patio. On display are farming and cooking implements, a wine press and a small exhibition on island architecture. There's also an informative section relating to Lanzarotean wine-making, and a few workshops where craftspeople such as carpenters, leatherworkers and basketweavers sometimes give demonstrations. There is an authentic tapas bar and a downstairs restaurant that serves Canarian lunches.

THE BASICS

www.centrosturisticos.com

✚ D5

✉ 11km (7 miles) northwest of Arrecife, near Mozaga

☎ 928 52 01 36

🕐 Daily 10–6

🍴 Restaurant and bar-café

🚌 20

♿ Good

💲 Free

HIGHLIGHTS

● Cubist monument
● Museum of rural culture
● Canarian tapas bar and restaurant

TIP

● The monument features on many tours as it lies at a crossroads with Arrecife to the south, La Geria to the west, Tinajo and Famara to the north, and Teguise and Tahíche to the east.

Museo Agrícola El Patio

TOP 25

The old farm still survives in its original form and includes a restored windmill

THE BASICS

- ⊕ D5
- ✉ C/ Echeyde 18, Crta Sóo-Tiagua (17km/10.5 miles northwest of Arrecife)
- ☎ 928 52 91 34
- 🕐 Mon–Fri 10–5.30, Sat 10–2.30
- 🍴 Bar-café
- 🚌 16
- ♿ Few
- 💰 Inexpensive

HIGHLIGHTS

- Farmhouse exhibition
- Restored windmills
- *Bodegón*

TIP

- Kids used to modern, interactive museums may find the exhibition fusty; take them out to meet the livestock instead.

Situated within a working farm, this modest country museum does a great job of evoking the atmosphere of Lanzarote's rural past through old photographs and displays of vintage tools.

El Patio estate El Patio has been cultivated since 1845 and is one of the oldest existing Lanzarotean farms; many were destroyed in the volcanic eruptions in 1730s. The land around Tiagua lies just beyond the limit of the lava fields and is therefore fertile, enriched with nutrients supplied by volcanic ash. Over the course of a century, the farm became the largest on the island, employing 25 labourers and over 20 camels.

Today The estate now includes orchards, tomato and cereal fields, and vineyards producing Moscatel, Malvasía and Lanzarotean red wine. The museum is a low-key sideline to this activity: the grand old farmhouse has been converted into an exhibition space where you can browse interesting photos of peasant life. You can also visit the farm-workers' quarters at the back, which have been furnished as they would have been a century or so ago. Outside, in the flower-filled patio, are a pair of carefully restored and maintained windmills —a classic, cone-topped *molino,* its sails mounted on a tower, and a *molina*, built on the roof of a flat-roofed building. There's also a characterful little wine museum stuffed with antique bottles, a traditional wine press, and a *bodegón* where you can knock back a glass of the house tipple with a little bread or artisan-made goat's cheese.

Parque Nacional de Timanfaya

HIGHLIGHTS

● Geothermal tricks
● Ruta de los Volcanes
● El Diablo
● Echadero de Camellos

TIPS

● Don't miss the visitor centre near Mancha Blanca (▷ 53).
● You can visit the camel station without paying the Montañas de Fuego entrance fee.

Lanzarote's brooding volcanoes and lava fields present a strange paradox. Silent and scorched, they have an eerie atmosphere, yet these new landscapes represent a fresh beginning, and they're already being colonized by living things.

Fire mountains Arguably the most impressive of Lanzarote's natural attractions, Timanfaya preserves the extraordinary landscapes created by the volcanic eruptions that began in 1730 and continued for six nerve-shattering years. During this time, 26 major explosions occurred, creating a chain of volcanoes stretching roughly east-west, surrounded by vast expanses of ash and twisted rock. Miraculously, very few injuries occurred and no lives were lost: The flow of lava was slow, with minimal release of toxic gases. Nonetheless,

Clockwise from far left: lichen and succulents thrive along the rope lava; a view across the landscape of the Parque Nacional de Timanfaya; El Diablo sign at the entrance; visitors take a camel ride; geothermal demonstrations on top of the volcano

villages, fields and livelihoods were destroyed, and Lanzarote took generations to recover.

Visiting the park The volcanoes are now dormant but in some areas the surface is too hot to walk on, so it's not possible to roam. Visitors converge on the Islote de Hilario in the Montañas del Fuego and are treated to graphic demonstrations of how hot the subterranean temperature can be: A warden throws some kindling into a fissure and it bursts into flames, then pours water into a gap, whereupon vapour blasts up like a geyser. The Ruta de los Volcanes tour (▷ 74) is, by contrast, a gentle experience—you admire the scene through coach windows to a musical soundtrack. There's also a geothermal restaurant (El Diablo ▷ 83). Finally, at the Echadero del Camellos, you can jump in the saddle for a camel ride.

THE BASICS

www.centrosturisticos.com

➕ B5

✉ 28km (17 miles) west of Arrecife

Montañas del Fuego

☎ 928 84 02 38

🕐 Daily 9–6 (to 5pm in winter); last tour at 1 hour before closing. Echadero de Camellos 9–4 (to 1pm in summer)

🍴 Restaurant 🚹 Good

💲 Moderate (includes Ruta del los Volcanes coach tour; camel rides extra)

Playa Blanca

In the space of a decade, Playa Blanca has mushroomed into a modern holiday resort, ribboning decoratively along the south coast, with views across the sparkling Bocaina Strait to Isla de Lobos and Fuerteventura.

Southern resort Next to nothing remains of the fishing hamlet that was once the only settlement in this area. In its place is a pleasant new town that's almost wholly devoted to tourism. Its relatively high concentration of modern, good-quality hotels and apartments attract more affluent visitors than the other resorts: Puerto del Carmen may have more bars and restaurants to choose from, but Playa Blanca wins out in the style stakes. Its facilities are also a big hit with young families. Right in the middle of the resort is Playa Dorada,

Sun, sea and sand on the beachfront at Playa Blanca (left); admiring the sea view (top right); Castillo de las Coloradas (bottom right)

a calm, sheltered beach with shallow waters, perfect for paddling and sandcastle-making, and nearby is Kikoland, a kids' entertainment complex, well set up for sports and organized activities.

Hugging the coast Playa Blanca is continuing to grow in leaps and bounds: new hotel complexes and a smart marina, the Marina Rubicón, now engulf the coastline, with large housing estates lined up behind them. However, the town, which is separated from the rest of the island by the arid slopes of Los Rostros, retains a remote and low-key atmosphere. An attractive seafront promenade, which is popular with walkers and cyclists, runs all the way from the Pechiguera lighthouse on the west side of town to the 18th-century Castillode las Coloradas at Punta de Águila, and east to Las Coloradas.

THE BASICS

➕ B8

✉ 38km (23.5 miles) southwest of Arrecife

🍴 Restaurants, cafés and bars

🚌 6

⛴ Ferry to Corralejo, Fuerteventura (11–13 sailings daily; 20 min; ▷ 117)

ℹ El Varadero, tel 928 51 90 18

Playa Grande

● Beach cafés
● Avenida de las Playas

● Playa Grande has shallow water and is safe for young children, but can get crowded during the peak season.
● Playa Chica is good for snorkelling.

Puerto del Carmen's prize asset is its long, sandy beach, decked out with blue-and-orange parasols and giant swan-shaped pedaloes, and backed by the buzzing Avenida de las Playas.

Grand sands Playa Grande certainly lives up to its name. Its main section, an unbroken stretch of broad, dark-gold sand, is over a kilometre long. Beyond this there are more beaches, each with a different character: the small, sheltered Barrilla and Chica beaches to the east and, to the west, some picturesque rocky coves and the huge, quiet Playa de los Pocillos. All receive plenty of good weather —Puerto del Carmen typically scores record numbers of sunshine-hours per year—and offer good swimming in the summer months, particularly between late July and mid-September. To add to

The main palm-fringed beach at Playa Grande (left) and to the west, a watchtower at Playa Los Picillos (right)

the holiday appeal, there's watersports kit to rent and banana boat rides or parasailing to try. The nearby scuba operators run training courses and trips, and rent out snorkelling gear.

Avenida de las Playas The beaches lie at the foot of a low cliff, along the top of which runs a broad promenade fringed with palm trees and scarlet hibiscus. This follows the course of the Avenida de las Playas, Puerto del Carmen's hectic Strip—a long parade of resort-style cafés, bars, restaurants and shops, which becomes less concentrated the further north you go, finally petering out at the end of the beach. There are a couple of cafés on the promenade with tables looking out over the sand and the sea, particularly good for a lunchtime sandwich or an afternoon ice cream while you lap up the sun and the view.

THE BASICS

➕ D7
✉ Avda Playas, Puerto del Carmen
🍴 Restaurants, cafés and bars
🚌 2, 3

Punta de Papagayo

The unspoilt and uncrowded coves of Punta de Papagayo

THE BASICS

🔲 B8

✉ East of Playa Blanca; 37km (23 miles) southwest of Arrecife

🍴 Café

🅿 Car parking inexpensive

HIGHLIGHTS

● Playa Mujeres
● Playa del Pozo
● Playa del Papagayo
● Puerto Muelas

TIP

● Several boat operators include Papagayo in their itineraries, anchoring close to shore for swimming and snorkelling.

If you like beaches that are unspoilt, undeveloped and refreshingly uncrowded, you're likely to love the Punta de Papagayo headland in the far south of the island.

Los Ajaches The rugged desert east of Playa Blanca and south of Puerto del Carmen and Puerto Calero, La Reserva Natural Protegido de los Ajaches is protected for its geological interest. The landscape may at first appear rather monotonous, but it's a popular area for desert rambles. At the southern tip of this region is a headland, the Punta de Papagayo, that looks as if bites have been taken out of it, leaving sandy beaches behind. These beaches are a little hard to get to —from Playa Blanca, count on a walk of at least 45 minutes, or a dusty drive along the graded track through the nature reserve—but well worth the effort. All have clean, pale sand lapped by turquoise water. It's a good idea to bring your own shade, water and supplies; there's just one café, on the edge of the headland car park. This serves drinks and snacks and has a few tables overlooking Playa del Papagayo.

The beaches The largest Papagayo beach is Playa Mujeres, nearest Playa Blanca; next to this is Playa del Pozo, and then the most famous beach, Playa del Papagayo, a small, horseshoe-shaped cove surrounded by sheer cliffs. The next beach, Puerto Muelas, is quieter and clothing-optional. All can be reached via sandy tracks that lead down from the car park.

Colourful gardens and pristine houses, set the scene at Yaiza

TOP
25

Yaiza

The pretty village of Yaiza has splendid views of the Timanfaya volcanoes. In the 18th century, it escaped the flow of lava by a whisker, and came to be regarded as a place of great spiritual significance.

Peaceful village Yaiza is a district capital—but you'd hardly guess from its modest size and sleepy atmosphere. Its pristine streets of whitewashed houses are arranged around a small, shady central church square, Plaza de los Remedios. Jaunty pots of geraniums lend a splash of colour here and there but there's an over-whelming sense of nothing much going on, making Yaiza a supremely peaceful place for a short stroll. The oldest part of the village is a cluster of farm buildings whose painstaking restoration was overseen by César Manrique. Passionate about tra-ditional architecture, Yaiza was one of his favourite spots, and he helped give the farm new life as a highly regarded Canarian restaurant called La Era (▷ panel, 84). While few other 18th-century buildings remain, Yaiza has several fine 19th-century houses, originally built as the homes of prosperous merchants.

Catholic tradition Yaiza has a strong Catholic tradition and is the focus of an important *romería*, or pilgrimage, marking the Fiesta de Nuestra de Señora de los Remedios on 8 September. Islanders dressed in traditional costume take part in the festivities, and after the solemn ceremonies there are treasure hunts for the kids, followed by folk music and dancing.

THE BASICS

✚ B6
✉ 23km (14 miles) west of Arrecife
🍴 Restaurants and café-bars
🚌 6

HIGHLIGHTS

● Village architecture
● Volcano views

Valle de la Geria

TOP 25

HIGHLIGHTS

- Vineyard views
- Winery tours
- Museo del Vino El Grifo

TIP

- Organized tours of central Lanzarote usually include a visit to the wineries, with tastings.

The volcanic winelands of La Geria, where emerald green vines thrive in fields of black lava, are extraordinary. Both beautiful and functional, they've been described as a perfect synthesis of art and engineering.

Ancient art Lanzaroteans have been making wine for at least 500 years, and sweet, fruity Malavasía was a favourite of the European aristocracy in the 16th and 17th centuries. But when Timanfaya erupted, ruining the island's most fertile valleys, there was a lengthy hiatus in production. Eventually, the ingenious islanders began experimenting with new methods. They observed that *picón*—gravel composed of small, light, pitted pieces of lava—trapped the morning dew so effectively that a plant surrounded by this substance

The El Grifo Museo del Vino, located in the winelands of the Valle de la Geria, is full to the brim with interesting displays of anything that relates to wine

could survive long periods of drought. They also discovered that by planting individual vines in shallow depressions, each one sheltered by a low, crescent-shaped wall (*zoco*), they could protect them from the scorchingly salty prevailing winds.

Touring the wineries The valley of La Geria, in the foothills of Timanfaya, is home to several wineries, some of which are open to the general public for tastings and tours. The bumpy road that used to wind its way through La Geria from Uga to Mozaga has now been replaced by smooth tarmac, diluting the romance of the region but making it more accessible. The oldest winery, El Grifo, has a small museum. You can also visit Bodega La Geria, one of the largest, and Stratus, the newest, a high-end, state-of-the-art operation that looks set to raise the profile of Lanzarotean wine.

THE BASICS

✚ C6
✉ 19km (12 miles) west of Arrecife
🍴 Restaurants and bodegas
🍷 Tastings inexpensive

Museo del Vino El Grifo
www.elgrifo.com
✚ C5
✉ C/ La Geria (LZ-30), near Masdache
☎ 928 52 49 51
🕐 Daily 10.30–6
🍷 Museum inexpensive; winery tour expensive

ERMITA DE LOS DOLORES

This large village chapel may look rather plain from the outside, but it's an important Catholic shrine with a richly robed statue of the Virgin Mary. Legend has it that in 1735 a miracle, attributed to the Virgin, saved the village of Mancha Blanca from being engulfed by lava. The region celebrates on 15 September each year with a huge *romería* (Catholic pilgrimage) followed by a fiesta and rural craft fair.

➕ D5 ✉ Mancha Blanca, 25km (15.5 miles) northwest of Arrecife 🚌 16 ♿ Few 🎟 Free

FEMÉS

Perched high up on a saddle in the ancient Ajaches mountains, Femés, an attractive little village with a traditional feel, has commanding views over the Rubicón desert. On clear days there are also good views of Playa Blanca and Montaña Roja, the extinct volcano at the island's southwestern tip, and across the Bocaina Strait to Fuerteventura, its dunes standing

out as a strip of creamy white.

➕ B7 ✉ 25km (15.5 miles) southwest of Arrecife 🍴 Restaurants and café-bars 🚌 5

LOS HERVIDEROS

On the southwestern shore just south of Timanfaya, close to the road from El Golfo to the Salinas de Janubio, are Los Hervideros (the boiling pots). This system of volcanic inlets and blowholes can be highly impressive in stormy weather, when water crashing against the petrified lava is propelled high into the air.

➕ A6 ✉ 30km (19 miles) west of Arrecife

MUSEO AERONÁUTICO

www.aena.es

This new aviation museum makes good use of Lanzarote's old terminal building, operational from 1946 to 1970, the dawn of the island's mass-market tourist industry. On show are photos, documents, navigational instruments and models of planes, but the prize exhibit is a magnificent acrylic mural by César Manrique

Ermita de los Dolores

Los Hervideros, with Timanfaya National Park in the background

dating back to 1953. It depicts a colourful impression of island life, with cheerful-looking peasants and camels in a landscape of volcanoes, palms and fishing villages.

➕ E6 ✉ Aeropuerto de Lanzarote
☎ 928 84 63 65 🕐 Mon–Sat 10–2 🚌 22, 23 ♿ Good ✋ Free

PUERTO CALERO

www.puertocalero.com

A little west of Puerto del Carmen, this is one of Lanzarote's newest, and swishest, residential developments, focused on a modern marina. It's a refined spot with a couple of luxury hotels, a parade of designer shops and some good waterside places to eat and drink. It's also home to an interesting natural history museum devoted to the whales and dolphins found in this stretch of the Atlantic. Visitors can find out about cetacean ecology through watching documentaries, examining bones and listening to recordings of whale and dolphin calls. Marking the entrance to the museum is the impressive skeleton

of a Bryde's whale, mounted like a sculpture.

➕ C7 ✉ 19km (12 miles) west of Arrecife
🍴 Restaurants, cafés and bars

Museo de Cetáceos de Canarias

www.museodecetaceos.org

☎ 928 84 95 60 🕐 Tue–Sat 10–6
♿ Good ✋ Expensive

PUERTO DEL CARMEN

Lanzarote's first tourist resort is still the island's biggest, though Playa Blanca seems determined to catch up. Pleasantly low-rise, it's a ribbon development of neat little villas and apartment buildings overlooking a long stretch of sun-drenched beach (▷ 62–63). Its main drag, the Avenida de las Playas, is somewhat tacky, lined with souvenir shops and rowdy bars, but modernization plans are in progress. In the old fishing quarter, La Tiñosa, a tourist village of restaurants and bars have replaced the cottages and boathouses that used to cluster around the harbour.

➕ D7 ✉ 16km (10 miles) west of Arrecife
🍴 Restaurants, cafés and bars 🚌 2, 3, 6

Yellow submarine motoring out of the marina at Puerto Calero

The harbour at Puerto del Carmen

SALINAS DE JANUBIO

www.salinasdejanubio.com

Salt was once an important export commodity for the Canaries. This is the last survivor of its kind in the archipelago, where you can see the striking geometry and hues of Lanzarote's largest commercial salt pans.

✚ B7 ✉ 30km (19 miles) west of Arrecife

SAN BARTOLOMÉ

The dignified old town of San Bartolomé is little visited by tourists despite being an excellent place to soak up the atmosphere of authentic Lanzarote. In its centre is an attractive church square—the kind of place where pensioners in felt trilbies sit in the shade to swap news with their neighbours—and a local history museum crammed with artefacts relating to island life in the 19th and 20th centuries.

✚ E6 ✉ 10km (6 miles) northwest of Arrecife 🍴 Restaurants, bars and cafés 🚌 16, 20

Museo Etnográfico Tanit

www.museotanit.com

✉ C/ Constitución 1 ☎ 928 52 06 55
🕐 Mon–Sat 10–2 ♿ Good 💰 Moderate

LA SANTA

Synonymous with sport, the northwestern village of La Santa is dominated by its Centro Deportivo, Club La Santa (▷ 110), a residential complex catering for both professional athletes despatched here for intensive training sessions and enthusiastic amateurs. Club La Santa is also the base for the annual Ironman triathlon (▷ panel, 77).

✚ D4 ✉ 26km (16 miles) northwest of Arrecife 🍴 Restaurants, cafés and bars 🚌 16

UGA

Though somewhat overshadowed by its better-known neighbour, Yaiza, Uga is a pretty little winemaking village on the edge of La Geria. Its name often crops up on the menus of smart restaurants as it is home to a smokehouse that produces delicious smoked salmon.

✚ C7 ✉ 21km (13 miles) west of Arrecife 🍴 Restaurants 🚌 6

Museo Tanit bell tower, San Bartolomé

Flowers adorn the courtyard of the church, Uga

A Walk Around Arrecife

Arrecife oozes local flavour, and its attractive seafront promenade, commercial district and old quarters are easy to explore on foot.

DISTANCE: 5km (3 miles)   **ALLOW:** 2 hours

START

KIOSO DE LA MÚSICA
 c3

END

KIOSO DE LA MÚSICA

1 From the timber and lava-stone bandstand, walk along the promenade with the sea on your right, toward the Castillo de San Gabriel. Cross the Puenta de las Bolas to visit the fort.

2 Back on the promenade, continue northeast then turn inland along C/ Manuel Miranda to make a stop at La Recova, the restored marketplace, which is on the right.

3 Further on is Plaza de las Palmas and the Iglesia de San Ginés. With the church behind you, go right and right again to follow the white-washed lanes to El Charco de San Ginés.

4 A pleasant promenade and a bridge across the mouth of the lagoon allow you to make a complete circuit.

8 To find your way back to the starting point, keep walking west along the promenade to Avenida La Maraina.

7 Continue along the parallel back-streets of C/ Riego or C/ Luis Morote until you're back on the main seafront road, Avda Dr. Rafael González. There's plenty of places to eat and drink along the seafront, most with great views.

6 This leads to C/ León y Castillo, the main shopping street. Turn west along C/ Quiroga, which is pedestrianized, with pavement cafés.

5 At the inland end of the lagoon, take one of the lanes that leads west.

A Walk Along the Ruta de Tremesana

Timanfaya is off-limits to casual hikers, why not sign up for this free guided walk, hosted by a knowledgeable national park warden.

DISTANCE: 3.5km (2 miles)   **ALLOW:** 2.5–3 hours

START ······· **END**

CENTRO DE VISITANTES E INTERPRETACIÓN

✚ C5 ⏰ Mon, Wed, Fri am; advance booking required, tel 928 84 08 39

CENTRO DE VISITANTES E INTERPRETACIÓN

❶ Having met up with the guide at the Centro de Visitantes (▷ 53), you and the rest of the party take a short minibus ride to the start of the route, near the foot of Montaña Tremesana.

❼ The walk comes to a close with another short minibus trip back to the Centro de Visitantes.

❷ Near the beginning of the route you'll be able to take a look inside a lava cave to view the molten appearance of the rock, stained yellow with sulphur.

❻ At this point, the guide will point out spots in the near distance where a shimmer of heat haze shows that the subterranean temperature is still extremely high.

❸ As you pass Caldera Rajada, you'll learn how this volcano erupted from the side and some of the resulting lava channels still remain as hollow tubes.

❹ There are interesting examples of cultivation at various points on the walk, including vines and fig trees, clinging to life in areas where fertile soil is covered with a thin layer of water-retaining lava gravel.

❺ Continuing past Volcán Hernández and Volcán Encantada, you can examine the beginnings of natural plant growth, including succulents, grasses and various lichen species.

A Drive Around Southern Lanzarote

This loop takes you through attractive villages, mountains and wine-lands—if you're staying in Playa Blanca pick up the trail at stage 4.

DISTANCE: 73km (45 miles)   **ALLOW:** 4 to 8 hours

START

PUERTO DEL CARMEN
✚ D7

1 From the lively beach resort of Puerto del Carmen (▷ 62–63, 69), drive towards Mácher, then follow the main road (LZ-2) west, in the direction of Yaiza.

2 After 7km (4 miles), turn left at the roundabout to take the mountain road to Femés (▷ 68). On a clear day, stop to enjoy a drink or some lunch while admiring the views.

3 Head down the steep and winding road that crosses the Rubicón plain to Playa Blanca (▷ 60–61), another possible lunch stop.

4 The seafront promenade and the Marina Rubicón are both pleasant places to stroll. If you'd like to visit an unspoilt beach, make a diversion to Punta del Papagayo (▷ 64).

END

PUERTO DEL CARMEN

8 Drive southwest past the mighty Montaña Blanca, one of the highest peaks in the south, to Tías, and back to Puerto del Carmen.

7 The road leads on to Manrique's striking Campesino monument and museum (▷ 55). At the Campesino roundabout, turn right toward San Bartolomé, home to the Tanit museum (▷ 70).

6 After 13km (8 miles) turn right at the roundabout to the village of Yaiza (▷ 65). From Yaiza, rejoin the main Arrecife road. At Uga (▷ 70), turn left onto the LZ-30 for La Geria (▷ 66–67), to explore the wineries.

5 Leave Playa Blanca by the main road (LZ-2) north.

A Drive Around Timanfaya

Timanfaya has stupendous views, and this trip includes the Ruta de los Volcanes coach tour, the only way to see the heart of the park.

DISTANCE: 60km (37 miles) **ALLOW:** 4 hours

START

END

CENTRO DE VISITANTES E INTERPRETACIÓN ➕ C5

CENTRO DE VISITANTES E INTERPRETACIÓN

1 Start by soaking up some background information on the region at the Centro de Visitantes (▷ 53).

8 Back on the main Timanfaya road, keep heading northwest to drive through more lava fields to the Centro de Visitantes.

2 Drive toward Mancha Blanca then turn right to take the scenic LZ-56, which heads across the lava fields between Montaña de los Rostros and Caldera Quemada, and continues past Montaña Ortiz and Montaña Negra.

7 To take a ride on a camel, stop at the Echadero de Camellos, on the left as you approach the Montañas del Fuego. A bit further on, turn left to drive up to Islote de Hilario and join the excellent Ruta de los Volcanes tour.

3 Turn right along the LZ-30 to admire the southern La Geria winelands (▷ 66–67), an ingenious use of the volcanic landscape.

6 Rejoin the LZ-2 heading east. On the north side of Yaiza, turn left toward the Montañas del Fuego (▷ 58–59), marked by one of Manrique's impish devil signs. Timanfaya rises in the distance.

4 Turn right onto the main road (LZ-2) and bypass Yaiza (▷ 65), driving alongside the rugged lava fields at the southern limit of the park, toward El Golfo (▷ 54).

5 Double back, or make a coastal detour via Los Hervideros (▷ 68) and the Salinas de Janubio (▷ 70).

Shopping

BIOSFERA PLAZA

Puerto del Carmen's main shopping centre, a fairly modern, middle-market mixture of shops selling high-street fashions, sportswear and gadgets, is always busy with locals and tourists. It's located uphill from the Old Town on Calle Juan Carlos I.

🔢 D7 ✉ Puerto del Carmen 🚌 2, 3, 6

CALLE LEÓN Y CASTILLO

Arrecife's principal shopping district is a pleasant low-key pedestrian area with a good mixture of old-fashioned and up-to-the-minute shops, but very few big names. Look out for Fiammetta, a great little boutique selling eccentric clothes, bags and jewellery, which is just off the main drag at Calle Inspector Luís Martín 3.

🔢 b4–b3 ✉ Arrecife 🚌 1, 2, 5, 6, 7, 9, 10, 14, 16, 19, 20, 21, 23

MARINA RUBICÓN

The developers of Playa Blanca's upmarket marina had high hopes for it as a swanky, smart

---

WINERY SHOPS

One of the best places to buy wine on the island is the Casa-Museo del Campesino (▷ 55), which has a good selection from all the best bodegas. However, if you've discovered a preference for a particular winery, it makes sense to buy direct. There's a particularly helpful shop at El Grifo (▷ 67), famous for its superbly smooth *semidulce* and Moscatel.

---

shopping centre; at the time of writing, these seem to be faltering, with many of the outlets empty, but you'll still find a few attractive places selling quality clothing and gifts; there's also a great contemporary art gallery in a building designed to resemble a village church.

🔢 B8 ✉ Playa Blanca 🚌 6

PUERTO CALERO

As at Marina Rubicón, the handful of designer shops at this upmarket site are generally pretty quiet, making it a relaxing place to browse for designer labels such as La Perla, Tommy Hilfiger, Ralph Lauren and Custo, followed by a drink or a bite at one of the prosperous quayside bars and restaurants.

🔢 C7 ✉ Puerto Calero

Entertainment and Activities

4 LUNAS

Cuatro Lunas, part of the pleasant collection of venues run by the Hotel Princesa Yaiza is a cocktail bar and nightspot for grownups, with live jazz (piano, vocals or a band) on Thursdays, Fridays and Saturdays.

🔢 B8 ✉ Pl Princesa Yaiza, Playa Blanca ☎ 928 51 92 22 🕐 Tue–Sat 8pm–3am 🚌 6

ATLÁNTICA CENTRO DE BUCEO

www.atlanticadiving.es
This PADI training centre offers scuba lessons and certification courses at all levels. Classroom facilities at its base are located in the Hotel Los Fariones, right on the beach.

🔢 D7 ✉ C/ Acatife 2, Puerto del Carmen ☎ 928 51 07 17 🚌 2, 3, 6

BIOSFERA

Lanzarote's only megaclub, near the seafront on the south side of town, has giant sound systems and room for 2,500 party people under an open-sided dome. Special events featuring international DJs are sometimes staged here, including big celebrations during the city's San Ginés festivities

in the summer.

🎵 Off map at a2   ✉ Avda Fred Olsen, Arrecife   ☎ 928 82 41 98   🕐 Thu–Sat from midnight   🚌 1, 2, 5, 6, 7, 9, 10, 14, 16, 19, 20, 21, 23

BUDDY'S

www.buddyslanzarote.com
Small live music venue with a refreshingly genuine feel and a mixed programme of rock, punk, blues, soul and jazz. In the heart of Puerto del Carmen's Old Town.

🎵 D7   ✉ C/ Tenerife 18, Puerto del Carmen   🕐 Tue–Sat 9.30pm–2am   🚌 2, 3, 6

CAFÉ LA OLA

www.cafelaolalanzarote.com
This all-day chillout venue makes a good attempt at bringing contemporary style to the Strip with an Ibiza-esque pool terrace and a mellow bar-restaurant decked out with cushions and Buddhas. Choose from a menu of light, Asian-inspired nibbles and designer cocktails.

🎵 D7   ✉ Avda de las Playas 41, Puerto del Carmen   ☎ 928 51 50 81   🕐 Daily 11am–3.30am   🚌 2, 3, 6

CAFÉ DEL CARMEN

This first-floor meeting place has a breezy terrace with great sea views, a free WiFi hotspot, and an all-day menu of drinks and snacks. Lounge and house DJs spin contemporary tunes to ensure an upbeat mood.

🎵 D7   ✉ CC Los Dragos

23–34, Avda Playas, Puerto del Carmen   ☎ 928 51 25 70   🕐 Daily till late   🚌 2, 3, 6

CAFÉ DEL MAR

The famous Ibizan brand may have lost the soul it started out with back in the 1990s, but the soundtrack of classic lounge beats at this rather pricey café-bar are as reliable as ever.

🎵 B8   ✉ Marina Rubicón, Playa Blanca   ☎ 928 34 92 00   🕐 Daily 10am–2am   🚌 6

CANARIAS YACHT CHARTER

www.canariasyachtcharter.com
Set sail in an ocean-going yacht to explore the Atlantic Ocean around Lanzarote, Fuerteventura and the Chinijo Archipelago. If you'd like to take it easy, indulge yourself and hire a skipper and hostess to look

---

LANZAROTE IRONMAN

Superfit athletes converge on La Santa each May to take part in the Lanzarote Ironman, one of the toughest triathlons on the world circuit. Many of the serious-looking runners, cyclists and swimmers you see on the island at other times of year are training for this key event. The challenge consists of a 3.8km (2.5-mile) swim in the sea, a 180km (111-mile) bike race and a 42.2km (26-mile) run.

---

after you on board.

🎵 C7   ✉ Puerto Calero   ☎ 620 61 55 50

CATLANZA

www.catlanza.com
This company runs group excursions from Puerto Calero to Punta del Papagayo by luxury sailing catamaran. The day includes lunch and the use of jetskis and snorkelling gear. Guests can also have a go at crewing. You can choose between a family trip or an adults-only option, with a champagne cocktail.

🎵 C7   ✉ Local 1, Puerto Calero   ☎ 928 51 30 22

GALERÍA DEL SOL

This small, characterful and perennially popular pub is positioned right in the thick of things.

🎵 B8   ✉ Avda Marítima 34, Playa Blanca   ☎ 928 51 75 05   🕐 Daily 11am–5am   🚌 6

GO-KARTING SAN BARTOLOMÉ

At this fun centre you can race your mates around a competition-standard track, hurtling along at up to 80kph (50mph). The centre includes dedicated tracks for kids aged 12–16 and 5–12 years. Everyone can then refuel on snacks or ice cream at the bar-restaurant. If you have a group of six or more you can book a pick-up from your accommodation free of charge.

🎵 E6   ✉ San Bartolomé   ☎ 928 52 00 22   🚌 16, 20

GRAN KARTING CLUB LANZAROTE

www.grankarting.com

Compete against your mates on this competition-standard karting track, and then toast your success at the bar-restaurant. There are also tracks specifically for kids aged 12–16 and 5–12 years.

➕ D6   ✉ La Rinconada, Tías (off the LZ-2, near the airport) ☎ 619 75 99 46 🚌 5, 6

HARLEY'S BAR

This hardcore hangout hosts live rock and metal bands at least four nights a week, and promises a free air guitar for every customer of its rock-karaoke sessions.

➕ B8   ✉ CC Papagayo, Playa Blanca ☎ 928 51 96 07 🕐 Daily 1pm–3am 🚌 6

HELICOPTEROS INSULARES

www.helicopterosinsulares.com

This Tenerife-based helicopter charter company covers the whole archipelago, offering aerial safaris over Lanzarote on request.

✉ Aeropuerto Reina Sofía, Tenerife ☎ 609 94 22 30

ISLAND WATERSPORTS DIVE CENTRE

www.divelanzarote.com

A British-run diving outfit that offers the full range of PADI courses plus BSAC training. Absolute beginners can take the plunge with a safe and easy 'try a dive' session,

or join a snorkelling tour from Puerto Calero, with all equipment provided.

➕ C7   ✉ Local 4, Puerto Calero ☎ 928 51 18 80

JUNGLE BAR

www.junglelanzarote.com

Playa Blanca's liveliest nightspot has an outdoor terrace for daytime drinking, and an indoor dance floor that gets moving in the early hours. The resident DJs attract a cheerful crowd of twenty-to-forty-somethings.

➕ B8   ✉ CC Papagayo 3, Playa Blanca ☎ 928 51 83 32 🕐 Daily 11am–5am 🚌 6

LANZA AIR

For unforgettable views of Lanzarote's volcanoes from above, this company will zoom you around in a light aircraft. Tours last over an hour and operate daily except Thursdays.

CANARY TREKKING

If you'd like to explore the island's rugged volcanic landscapes on foot but would rather not set out on your own, a great option is to join a guided hike with Canary Trekking (www.canarytrekking.com, ☎ 609 53 76 84). They run an easy-going, three-hour, 6km (3.5-mile) walk through the Parque Natural de los Volcanes, fringing Timanfaya. Alternatively, book a place on the Ruta de Tremesana (▷ 72), which is free.

There's room for three passengers on board.

➕ b2   ✉ C/ Juan Rejón 3, Arrecife ☎ 928 80 62 15 🚌 1, 2, 5, 6, 7, 9, 10, 14, 16, 19, 20, 21, 23

LANZABUGGY AVENTURA

www.lanzabuggy.com

Why not set off on a fun dune buggy tour of the volcanoes, badlands and salt pans, travelling by country roads and off-road tracks, and getting very dusty in the process.

➕ B8   ✉ C/ Breca 12, Playa Blanca ☎ 928 34 97 08 🚌 6

MA DIVING

www.madiving.com

This company takes divers out to famous local sites including the wrecked vessels near Puerto del Carmen, and The Cathedral, a large submarine lava cave where you can pick out eagle rays and moray eels by torchlight.

➕ D7   ✉ C/ Juan Carlos I, 35 Local 1, Puerto del Carmen ☎ 928 51 69 15 🚌 2, 3, 6

MAREA

A fabulous addition to Playa Blanca's cocktail scene, this beachfront bar with a cool, sleek, sophisticated atmosphere is a great spot for sundowners and snacks. After dark, the DJ turns up the volume on the funky indoor dancefloor.

➕ B8   ✉ CC/ La Mulata, Playa Blanca ☎ 928 51 99 19

🕐 Daily 10am–3.30am
🚌 6

MARINA RUBICÓN DIVING CENTER

www.rubicondiving.com
This extremely well-equipped dive school and centre offers masses of training options, including nitrox, rebreather and the National Geographic diving programme. There are daily trips for qualified divers, including visits to the sites around Isla de Lobos.

➕ B8 ✉ Marina Rubicón 77B, Playa Blanca ☎ 928 34 93 46 🚌 6

MEGAFUN

www.megafun-lanzarote.com
This established outfit offers island tours by quad bike or dune buggy, and rents out motorbikes.

➕ D7 ✉ CC Costa Mar, Pocillos, Puerto del Carmen ☎ 928 51 28 93 🚌 2, 3, 6

RUBICAT

www.marinarubicon.com
This catamaran excursion company runs similar trips as Catlanza (▷ 77), sailing to Punta del Papagayo for a pleasant day of swimming and snorkelling, but starting from Marina Rubicón.

➕ B8 ✉ Marina Rubicón, Playa Blanca ☎ 928 51 90 88 🚌 6

SAFARI DIVING

www.safaridiving.com
Well-established outfit in a convenient spot, with easy access to some of the best nearby sites. Playa Chica itself is sheltered and safe, making it a great place for beginners to go through the basics before heading out to more challenging waters.

➕ D7 ✉ Playa de la Barilla 4, Playa Chica, Puerto del Carmen ☎ 928 51 19 92 🚌 2, 3, 6

STARS BAR

Arrecife's only towerblock can't help but have the best views in the city— and this top floor bar is a smart spot from which to admire the scene. Music videos entertain after dark.

➕ a3 ✉ Arrecife Gran Hotel, Parque Islas Canarias, Arrecife ☎ 928 80 00 00 🕐 Daily till late 🚌 1, 2, 5, 6, 7, 9, 10, 14, 16, 19, 20, 21, 23

L'STRADA

Well-dressed locals chat, drink and dance in this ultramodern urban bar, a few paces from the sea-front in Arrecife.

➕ b3 ✉ C/ Riego 15, Arrecife ☎ No phone 🕐 Thu–Sat 11.30pm–5am 🚌 1, 2, 5, 6, 7, 9, 10, 14, 16, 19, 20, 21, 23

SUBMARINE SAFARIS

www.submarinesafaris.com
Specially designed for sightseeing with large portholes all the way along its hull, this yellow submarine takes groups of up to 44 people down to depths of 30m (98ft) to stare at the fish. Trips take place four times a day and last around an hour. A free bus picks you up from Costa Teguise and Puerto del Carmen.

➕ C7 ✉ Local 2, Puerto Calero ☎ 928 51 28 98

TROPICAL DELFÍN OCEAN CAT

www.oceancatt.com
Long-established sailing trip company, offering mini-cruises along the coast from Puerto del Carmen to Punta del Papagayo, Isla de Lobos and the northern coast of Fuerteventura, in a large sailing catamaran with a sun deck for carefree lounging. Lunch with drinks and the use of snorkelling gear and inflatables is included.

➕ D7 ✉ C/ Teide 30, Puerto del Carmen ☎ 928 51 23 23 🚌 2, 3, 6

Restaurants

AGUA VIVA (€€€)

Well worth the effort required to track it down, this impeccable little restaurant in an up-market suburb of Arrecife impresses with its fine ingredients and superb, haute-cuisine sauces. There are great ocean views from the terrace.

🔂 E6 ☒ C/ Mástil 31, Playa Honda ☎ 928 82 15 05 ⊙ Tue–Sat dinner only 🚌 2, 5, 6, 19, 21, 22, 23

ALMACÉN DE LA SAL (€€€)

www.almacendelasal.com
One of the best places to eat on the Playa Blanca seafront, with an old-fashioned atmosphere and quality fish and meat dishes.

🔂 B8 ☒ Avda Marítima 12, Playa Blanca ☎ 928 51 78 85 ⊙ Wed–Mon lunch, dinner 🚌 6

ALTAMAR (€€€)

Arrecife's five-star hotel has a suitably swish top-floor restaurant serving well-prepared European and international fare, with elegant service and stunning panoramic views of the city and the sea.

🔂 a3 ☒ Arrecife Gran Hotel, Parque Islas Canarias, Arrecife ☎ 928 80 00 00 ⊙ Daily lunch, dinner 🚌 1, 2, 5, 6, 7, 9, 10, 14, 16, 19, 20, 21, 23

AMURA (€€€)

www.restauranteamura.com
This upmarket show-stopper, housed in a sparklingly white quayside mansion with ocean views, has gained a growing reputation for imaginative dishes such as monkfish served with cuttlefish and limpets. It's the best place to eat in upmarket Puerto Calero.

🔂 C7 ☒ Puerto Calero ☎ 928 51 31 81 ⊙ Tue–Sun lunch, dinner

AROMAS YAIZA (€€€)

This is Playa Blanca's hidden gem, with an award-winning chef who produces beautiful rendi-tions of Canarian dishes such as *cherne* (a local fish) with prawns or marinated pork, served in elegant surroundings.

🔂 B6 ☒ C/ La Laja 1, Playa

Blanca ☎ 928 34 96 91 ⊙ Mon–Sat lunch, dinner 🚌 6

BODEGA (€€)

With the kind of warm, rustic appeal that's hard to find in Puerto del Carmen, this is a relaxed spot to enjoy traditional Spanish food and wine, a short walk from the bustle of the old harbour district.

🔂 D7 ☒ C/ Roque Nublo 3, Puerto del Carmen ☎ 928 51 29 53 ⊙ Daily lunch, dinner 🚌 2, 3, 6

LA BODEGA DE SANTIAGO (€€)

Wonderful rural restau-rant that breathes new life into historic recipes, including a succulent beef-and-peaches dish. On the Timanfaya side of Yaiza, it has a pleasant village setting, a leafy ter-race and a well-preserved vintage interior.

🔂 B6 ☒ C/ García Escámez 23, Yaiza ☎ 928 83 62 04 ⊙ Tue–Sun lunch, dinner 🚌 6

LA BODEGA DE UGA (€€€)

A pricey but highly convivial place for local wine—some of it from Uga—and tapas such as goat's cheese, cured meat and olives. Salmon cured in the smokehouse over the road is among the house specialties.

🔂 C7 ☒ LZ-2, Uga ☎ 928 83 01 47 ⊙ Mon–Wed, Fri–Sun lunch, dinner 🚌 6

81

EL BODEGÓN LOS CONEJEROS (€€)

Like a country wine-bar transported to the city, this smoky, but appealing, place on the seafront in central Arrecife serves hearty food and is hugely busy with locals at weekends.

⊞ b3 ⊠ Avda Rafael González Negrín 9, Arrecife ☎ 928 81 71 95 ◉ Mon–Sat dinner only ⬚ 1, 2, 5, 6, 7, 9, 10, 14, 16, 19, 20, 21, 23

BODEGÓN DE LAS TAPAS (€)

In a quiet section of the Playa Blanca seafront, this is a good place to munch your way through tasty portions of sardines, peppers, olives, sliced cured meat and salads.

⊞ B8 ⊠ Paseo Maritimo 5, Playa Blanca ☎ 928 51 83 10 ◉ Daily lunch, dinner ⬚ 6

LA CABAÑA (€€–€€€)

www.lacabana.com

A change from the usual, as the international dishes on the menu here, created by British chef Darren Spurr, are served with twist. Choose from the likes of caramelized pork fillet wtih Calvados or honey roast duck breast. Fresh fish is a specialty, too.

⊞ D7 ⊠ Crta Arrecife, Mácher ☎ 650 68 56 62 ◉ Tue–Sat from 7pm ⬚ 5, 6, 19

CASA EMILIANO (€)

The best place from which to enjoy Femés'

famous views across the Rubicón plain to Playa Blanca, over a leisurely lunch of simple local fare such as stews and grills.

⊞ B7 ⊠ C/ La Plaza 10, Femés ☎ 928 83 02 23 ◉ Tue–Sun lunch, dinner ⬚ 5

CASA ROJA (€€)

www.lacasaroja-lanzarote.com

Rather pricey, but classy, this quayside restaurant has a creative menu that makes good use of local favourites such as sea bass and snapper alongside more exotic ingredients such as spicy couscous and truffles.

⊞ B8 ⊠ Marina Rubicón, Playa Blanca ☎ 928 51 96 44 ◉ Daily lunch, dinner ⬚ 6

CASA SIAM (€€)

www.casasiam.com

One of the island's best Asian eateries, this authentic Thai serves up beautifully presented curries and rice dishes, in an atmospheric setting.

THE BEST BODEGAS

Many of Lanzarote's wineries have a bar where you can buy wine by the glass, and perhaps some bread, cheese, olives or chorizo to accompany it. In many towns and villages, you'll find urban bodegas that are like a cross between a wine bar and a restaurant: the emphasis is as much on fine food as fine wine.

⊞ D7 ⊠ CC La Peñita, Avda Playas 22, Puerto del Carmen ☎ 928 52 84 64 ◉ Daily lunch, dinner ⬚ 2, 3, 6

CASERÍO DE MOZAGA (€€€)

www.caseriodemozaga.com

Romantic rural restaurant with haute-cuisine dishes such as king prawns with orange or lamb with onion chutney, served in an elegant dining room. One of the finest places to dine on Lanzarote, with an excellent wine list.

⊞ E6 ⊠ C/ Malva 8, San Bartolomé ☎ 928 52 00 60 ◉ Mon–Thu dinner, Fri–Sun lunch, dinner ⬚ 16, 20

LA CASONA DE YAIZA (€€€)

www.casonadeyaiza.com

Attractive restaurant attached to a grand mansion on the outskirts of Yaiza, with excellent Mediterranean and Canarian cuisine.

⊞ B6 ⊠ C/ El Rincón, Yaiza ☎ 928 83 62 62 ◉ Mon, Tue lunch, dinner, Wed, Fri–Sun dinner only ⬚ 6

CASTILLO DE SAN JOSÉ (€€€)

Supremely stylish, this Manrique-designed restaurant is a favourite with power-lunching local executives. Manrique's cutting-edge interior is as impressive today as it was in the 1970s, while plate-glass windows offer big views of the port.

⊞ F6 ⊠ Avda de Naos, Arrecife ☎ 928 81 23 21

🔵 Daily lunch, dinner
🚌 1, 2, 5, 6, 7, 9, 10, 14, 16, 19, 20, 21, 23

EL CHUPADERO (€)
www.el-chupadero.com
With stunning views of the wine region, this small understated German-run bodega offers fresh tapas, hand-picked wines and a hip atmosphere.
➕ B6 ✉ C/ Guardilama 3, La Geria, Yaiza ☎ 928 17 31 15 🔵 Wed–Sun lunch, dinner

COSTA AZUL (€€)
Here you can take a beachside table to enjoy the sunset before tucking into a feast of fresh fish.
➕ B6 ✉ Avda Marítima 7, El Golfo ☎ 928 17 31 99 🔵 Daily lunch, dinner

DÉJÀ VU (€€)
Close to Puerto del Carmen but with a pleasantly rural feel, this comfortable, softly-lit restaurant offers tasty Spanish fare.
➕ D7 ✉ Crta Tías-Yaiza, Mácher ☎ 626 31 52 11 🔵 Tue–Sat lunch, dinner, Sun dinner only 🚌 5, 6, 19

EL DIABLO (€€)
A chicken leg cooked over a geothermal barbecue doesn't taste particularly special—but nonetheless, this famous Manrique-designed restaurant gets top marks for originality. It's a sleek, disc-shaped building inside the part of the national park for which an entry fee applies. The barbecue is open so you can watch the chefs in action before sitting down to lunch.
➕ C6 ✉ Islote de Hilario, Parque Nacional de Timanfaya ☎ 928 17 31 05 🔵 Daily 12–3.30

EMMAX (€€)
www.emmaxrestaurante.com
Delicious modern Italian cooking from a highly competent team. The menu changes daily and features fusion dishes such as marlin with *wasabi*, or pasta with salmon and langoustines.
➕ E6 ✉ Avda Playa Honda 21, Playa Honda ☎ 928 82 09 17 🔵 Daily lunch, dinner 🚌 2, 6, 19, 21, 22, 23

EL HORNO DE LA AGUELA (€€€)
A great choice if you're

CATCH OF THE DAY

Every one of Lanzarote's coastal towns has some kind of fish restaurant–some smart, some simple–but the best place for a blowout is El Golfo (▷ 54). Eating at one of this hamlet's waterfront restaurants is rarely cheap, especially if you request the house special, upon which the waiter will load up your table with whatever's freshest that day. Happily, though, it will be good quality fare that's never seen the inside of a freezer.

---

ravenous, this local-style place is famous for its rich and tasty roasted meat dishes.
➕ B8 ✉ C/ Tegala 10, Playa Blanca ☎ 928 51 78 25 🔵 Daily lunch, dinner 🚌 6

LILIUM (€€€)
www.liliumtias.com
Run by a wine expert who offers many wines by the glass and pairs them with superb food, this gastropub (more accurately, a wine bar) is highly recommended on all counts. The highly imaginative and ever-changing menu includes delights such as pork and banana kebabs or lamb with red curry, and fabulous desserts.
➕ D6 ✉ C/ Islote de Hilario 12, Tías ☎ 928 52 49 78 🔵 Mon–Sat lunch, dinner 🚌 5, 6, 19

MAR AZUL (€€)
A fine spot to enjoy extremely fresh fish and seafood. The sheltered first floor terrace has good views out to sea.
➕ B6 ✉ Avda Golfo 42, El Golfo ☎ 928 17 31 32 🔵 Daily lunch, dinner

MESÓN TIAGUA (€€€)
Unassuming from the outside, but run by a chef who cares deeply about quality food and artful presentation.
➕ D5 ✉ Avda Guanarteme 19, Tiagua ☎ 928 52 98 16 🔵 Mon, Wed–Sat dinner only, Sun lunch, dinner 🚌 16

MEZZA LUNA (€)

Relaxed, easy-going spot on the main road through Tinajo, offering above-average pizza and pasta at low prices.

🔢 D5 ✉ Avda Cañada 22, Tinajo ☎ 928 84 01 41 🕐 Daily lunch, dinner 🚌 16

O' BOTAFUMEIRO (€€€)

A good place to try Galician specialties such as Bilbao-style baby eels, cooked in garlic and spices, or turbot in white wine. For a real blow-out, you could try the seafood *parillada* (mixed platter).

🔢 D7 ✉ CC Costa Luz, C/ Alemania 9, Puerto del Carmen ☎ 928 51 15 03 🕐 Wed–Mon lunch, dinner 🚌 2, 3, 6

PINTXOS Y TAPAS (€€)

Highly tasty traditional tapas in a quiet area, near Playa Blanca's coolest bar, Marea (▷ 78).

🔢 B8 ✉ CC Mulata, Playa Blanca ☎ 928 51 86 84 🕐 Mon–Sat lunch, dinner 🚌 6

PUERTO BAHÍA (€€€)

Good views of the coast on the south side of Puerto del Carmen give this place the edge over the other restaurants in this part of town. There's a long menu of standards including grilled fish, meat, pizzas and pasta.

🔢 D7 ✉ Avda Varadero 5, Puerto del Carmen ☎ 928 51 37 93 🕐 Daily lunch, dinner 🚌 2, 3, 6

LA PUNTILLA (€€€)

The most sophisticated of Arrecife's lagoon-side places, this small, quiet restaurant offers delicious *bacalao*, langoustines and *revueltos* with chorizo.

🔢 d2 ✉ Ribera del Charco 52, Arrecife ☎ 928 81 60 42 🕐 Mon–Sat lunch, dinner 🚌 1, 2, 5, 6, 7, 9, 10, 14, 16, 19, 20, 21, 23

QUINTIN'S (€€€)

Smart, spacious restaurant with a contemporary feel and stylish, modern cooking to match.

🔢 D7 ✉ Avda Juan Carlos I, 25G, Puerto del Carmen ☎ 928 51 57 55 🕐 Mon–Sat dinner only 🚌 2, 3, 6

TABERNA DEL PUERTO (€€€)

While Puerto Calero is a thoroughly modern development, there's an

A NEW ERA?

One of Lanzarote's most famous restaurants, La Era, is currently closed, possibly permanently—a great disappointment to the many fans of its authentic Canarian cooking. The consolation is that its owner has another venture, La Tegala, which also offers superb local fare, but with a modern accent.
La Tegala
🔢 D7 ✉ Crta Tías-Yaiza 60, Mácher ☎ 928 52 45 24; www.lategala.com
🕐 Tue–Sat lunch, dinner, Mon dinner only 🚌 5, 6, 19

old-fashioned, authentic atmosphere to this down-to-earth eatery. It's great for classic tapas such as *pimientos de padrón*, stuffed courgettes or prawns with *jamón serrano*.

🔢 C7 ✉ Avda Marítima, Puerto Calero ☎ 928 51 28 82 🕐 Wed–Mon lunch, dinner

TABERNA STRELITZIA (€€)

This charming little restaurant specializes in Provençal-style cooking using superb cuts of meat; there's also a brilliant wine cellar. The lavishly decorated room upstairs is the perfect setting for a special celebration.

🔢 D5 ✉ Avda Guanarteme 55, Tiagua ☎ 928 52 98 41 🕐 Daily dinner only 🚌 16

TERRAZA PLAYA (€€)

The menu here offers no surprises but the location is great—on a quiet little cove, with the sea practically lapping your toes.

🔢 D7 ✉ Avda Playas 28, Puerto del Carmen ☎ 928 51 54 17 🕐 Daily lunch, dinner 🚌 2, 3, 6

EL TOMATE (€–€€)

The international menu at this popular restaurant in the old part of town includes sole fillet with baked baby calamares and noodles.

🔢 D7 ✉ C/ los Jameos ☎ 928 51 19 85 🕐 Daily lunch, dinner 🚌 2, 3, 6

Fuerteventura

Fuerteventura has a very different atmosphere from its northern neighbour. Its landscapes are older and dustier with a stark, spacious drama that grows on you, while its northeastern and southeastern beaches are first class, and a magnet for watersports enthusiasts.

Sights	88–100	Top 25	**TOP 25**
Drive	101	Betancuria ▷ **88**	
Shopping	102	Isla de Lobos ▷ **89**	
		Corralejo ▷ **90**	
Entertainment and Activities	102–105	La Oliva ▷ **92**	
		Península de Jandía ▷ **93**	
Restaurants	105–106	Parque Natural de las Dunas de Corralejo ▷ **94**	

Fuerteventura

Punta
la Herrad
Punta de
Tarajalito

Caleta Negra
Ajuy
Playa de
los Muertos
Playa de
la Solapa
Playa de
Garcey
Bla

Punta
Peñón Blanco
33
Entresala Fay
385
Punta del
Gavioto 360
Gavioto
Morro del
Tabaibejo
528
Playa Amanay
Punta Amanay
Sisacumb

Playa de
Terife 6
Playa Negras Chilegua Car
Playa de Ugán FV6

Punta de
Guadelupe **Las Herm**
Playa de
la Pared **La Pared**
**Urbanización
Panorama**
*Oasis
Park*
La L

Istmo de
la Pared Playas Matas Bla
**Costa
Calma**
Playa de Playa
Barlovento Barca
322 **Esmeralda
Loma Negra Jandía**
Playas de Sotavento
Playas de Jandía
**Casas de
Risco del Paso**
Risco del
Paso

Punta 812
Pesebre Playa de Pico de la Zarza
Punta de Cófete (Jandía)
Punta Barlovento **Cófete** 343
Pesebre 230 686 ▲ Degollada
Roque Fraile ▲ de Cófete **Monte
de Moro *Península de Jandía* del Mar**
**Urbanización
Esquinzo Marabu** Playa de Butihondo
■ **Puerto de
la Cruz**
Punta **Casas de
de Jandía Jorós** **Jandía
Playa**
**Morro
Jable**

0   5 km
0   3 miles

D   E   F   G   H
1 2 3 4 5 6 7 8 9

Punta Martiño
Playa de la Arena
Parque Natural del Islote de Lobos
Punta Gorda
Punta Lala
Isla de Lobos
127
La Caldera
El Puertito
Punta de los Lavaderos
271
Volcán de Bayuyo
Playa de la Calera
Flag Beach
Punta Blanca
Majanicho
Corralejo
Puerto Remedio
Punta de Tivas
FV101
Punta de Tostón o de la Ballena
Caleta del Río
Playa Bajo Negro
Playa de los Matos
Playa de Marfolín
El Roque
El Cotillo
Malpaís de Bayuyo
FV109
Parque Natural de las Dunas de Corralejo
Playa Alzada
FV1
Playa del Castillo
Playa del Aljibe de la Cueva
Ladera de la Mañita
Lajares
232
Playita del Poris
Playa de la Cabezuela
Playa del Águila
Punta de Taca
Playa de Esquinzo
309
La Blanca
La Lengua
421
Arena
Villaverde
314
Roja
Punta de Paso Chico
533
Caima
353
Ecanfraga
Playa de los Picachos
Casas del Jablito
Playa de Tebeto
399
Montaña Tindaya
387
Frontón
509
La Oliva
FV10
Parque Holandés
Punta del Tarajalito
Casas de las Llanadas
Playa de la Mujer
Monumento a Don Miguel de Unamuno
Vallebrón
689
Valle de Fimapaire
Morro Carnero
Caldereta
Playa de los Valdivias
Playa de Jarubio
El Malpaís Delgado Quemada
366
La Muda
Tindaya
La Matilla
El Time
511
Guisguey
Cabo del Agua
Playito del Charquito
251
Blanca
688
FV10
Cerro de Temejereque
Puerto Lajas
Los Molinos
FV221
Cerro de Aceituna
Ecomuseo de La Alcogida
Tefía
Tetir
Los Enstancos
Urbanización Rosa de la Monja
326
Tefía de Arriba
595
FV225
La Asomada
P I Risco Prieto
Majada Marcial
Playa de los Mozos
Atalaya de Risco Grande
Bermeja
Pico de la Fortaleza
439
Puerto del Rosario
Playa de Santa Inés el Valle
Embalse de los Molinos
417
Tao
Tesjuates
276
Las Veredas
Los Pozos
Llanos de la Concepción
FV30
FV207
542
Casillas del Ángel
Llano Pelado
Residencial Aguas Verdes
Casas de Almácigc
Campo
Llano del Sol
Valle de Santa Inés
La
596
483
666
Ampuyenta
Rosa del Taro
Morro Pinacho
El Matorral
19
tuno
Morro de la Fuente Vieja
Maninubre
FV413
Triquivijate
Nuevo Horizonte
670
Morro abaiba
724
FV674
Atalaya
Morro Janana
Antigua
417
Buenavista
Caleta de Fuste
etancuria
Valles de Ortega
Casas de Majada Blanca
193
Blanca de Abajo
FV2
ega de Palma
Agua de Bueyes
Casas de El Cortijo
Salinas del Carmen
708
Gran Montaña
FV20
Casillas de Morales
FV50
497
Playa del Muellito
Puerto de la Torre
uez
Pájara
Gairía
463
Tiscamanita
433
Casas de Pozo Negro
Playa de Leandro
Punta del Viento
erlas
608
Carbón
Cruz de Piedra
FV20
Playa Pozo Negro
Playa de los Vallichuellos
Tuineje
Malpaís Grande
439
Atalaya de Pozo Negro
Playa del Guincho
Playa de la Cueva
Las Casitas
354
Montañeta del Tamacite
242
435
FV2
Caldera de los Arrabales
398
Caldera de Jacomar
Punta de las Borriquilas
Tesejerague
FV512
Teguital
Morro del Peñós
Ensenada de Gran Valle
345
Tirba
FV2
Las Playitas
284
Morro del Cencerra
Playa de los James
Punta Entallada
467
Caracol
FV525
El Charco
Gran Tarajal
FV512
Playa del Pajarito
185
Entallada
ro de
atos
Giniginámar
Playa de los Pobres
Tarajalejo
Punta del Morrete
Playa de Agando
Punta del Caracol
ejo

J K L M

Betancuria

A windmill set beside the road to Betancuria (left); inside Casa Santa Maria (right)

THE BASICS

⊞ J5

✉ 28km (17 miles) south-west of Puerto del Rosario

🍴 Restaurants and bar-café

🚌 2

Iglesia-Catedral de Santa María de Betancuria

🕐 Mon–Fri 10.45–4.20, Sat 11–3.20

♿ Few 💶 Inexpensive

Casa Santa María Multivision

☎ 928 87 82 82

🕐 Mon–Sat 10–4

♿ Few 💶 Moderate

HIGHLIGHTS

● Iglesia-Catedral de Santa María de Betancuria
● Casa Santa María
● Lunch alfresco in the lovely church square

TIP

● Don't miss the Mirador de Morro Velosa, perched on a mountaintop a few kilometres north of Betancuria—a bar-café and exhibition space designed by César Manrique which has marvellous panoramic views.

A delightful spot for lunch, Betancuria is the prettiest of Fuerteventura's highland villages. Founded in the early 1400s by the island's European conquerors, there's a tangible sense of history in its striking church square.

Conqueror's refuge Betancuria takes its name from Jean de Béthencourt, the pioneering 15th-century colonialist, who believed that by siting his capital in a steep-sided valley, well hidden from the coast, it would be safe from Berber fortune-hunters. This turned out to be a false hope, but despite repeated raids by pirates and slavers, Betancuria remained the Fuerteventuran capital until 1834.

Cathedral church The village is pleasantly humble but its church, the grandly titled Iglesia-Catedral de Santa María de Betancuria, has an ostentatiously decorated interior. Rebuilt in the 17th century after Berbers destroyed the original building, it has several altars in various styles from naïve to baroque. On display is a collection of antique statuary, while to the left of the high altar is a vestry with an elaborately painted ceiling and an array of ecclesiastical vestments and silverware.

Living history Opposite the church is Casa Santa María, a 16th-century mansion that has been carefully restored and houses a good restaurant, a courtyard café, a craft shop and a cultural centre showing a very watchable audio-visual portrait of the island.

Isla de Lobos

Virtually uninhabited and protected as a nature reserve, Lobos is popular with wildlife-watchers. The island's clear waters are good for snorkelling and hikers may also see egrets, petrels, gulls and shearwaters wheeling overhead.

Island outpost The jagged, weathered remains of a volcanic eruption off the northeastern tip of Fuerteventura, Lobos is a small, barren island with just one tiny settlement, El Puertito, which has a harbourside fish restaurant and practically nothing else. It overlooks a natural lagoon with clear water for snorkelling. From here, it's a short walk to a sheltered beach, Playa de la Concha, perfect for swimming, although there's no shade.

Take a hike For something more energetic, hike to Montaña La Caldera, its crater half-collapsed into the sea, and climb to the top (127m/417ft) for superb views of both northern Fuerteventura and southern Lanzarote; alternatively, you could bring a mountain bike (and plenty of water) and tour the island's rugged waymarked pathways.

Wildlife Lobos is surrounded by submerged lava reefs and caves, making this a good destination for scuba divers. Underwater, you may encounter parrotfish, jacks, barracuda, sea urchins, and numerous other species; loggerhead turtles are also sometimes found. Despite the name, you won't see seals on the island—the monk seals (*lobos marineros*) after which it was named were wiped out by fishermen who saw them as competition.

THE BASICS

🟦 M1
🍽 Restaurant
🚢 Ferry from Corralejo (El Majorero; departs 10am and noon; returns 12.30 and 4pm; 10 min), or glass-bottom boat trip from Corralejo (Catamaran Celia Cruz; ▷ 102)
♿ None

HIGHLIGHTS

- Playa de la Concha
- Montaña La Caldera

TIP

- Several local scuba diving companies and boat operators running day trips to Corralejo from Playa Blanca (or vice versa) build a visit to Lobos into their itineraries.

Corralejo

TOP
25

HIGHLIGHTS

● Strolling around the Old Town
● Baku Family Park
● Glass-bottom boat trips to Isla de Lobos
● Ferry trips to Playa Blanca, Lanzarote

TIP

● Sandy beaches fringing the Parque Natural de las Dunas de Corralejo (▷ 94–95) are a heaven for kitesurfers, surfers and sun worshippers.

Fuerteventura's largest and northernmost resort—a short ferry-hop from Playa Blanca in Lanzarote—is a breezy spot with a lively, raffish Old Town and a sprawl of modern accommodation complexes within reach of some gorgeous beaches.

Old Corralejo The pleasant Old Town is the heart and soul of Corralejo: it's a cheerful jumble of narrow lanes lined with unpretentious bars, restaurants and ice cream shops. Its harbourside promenades overlook a string of white sandy coves where fishermen used to pull up their boats. While the fishing fleet is now much depleted, the port is still very active with yachts cruising in and out of the marina and ferries from Isla de Lobos (▷ 89) and Lanzarote docking at the main wharf.

Clockwise from far left: Monumento Al Marinero, a sculpture in the harbour; Waikiki tapas bar on Playa de los Verilitos; pleasure craft at the Corralejo harbour; yellow-legged gulls, a common sight on the harbour rocks; children fishing on the harbourfront with the resort visible beyond the bay; the modern Plaza de la Iglesia

Main Street Fringing the Old Town is a newer district whose high street, Avenida de Nuestra Señora de la Carmen, is home to offbeat boutiques, surf shops and banks. The surrounding streets, though scruffy, comprise a thriving commercial centre where you'll find untouristy shops, delis and places to eat and drink. A fun way to tour both the older and the newer parts of the town is to jump aboard the Tren de Alegría (Happy Train), a jaunty little tourist train costing €5 per circuit.

Holiday haven Further south, rapid development has crammed the Corralejo coast with row upon row of holiday homes and hotels. Among the shopping and entertainment complexes of the New Town is a family-friendly waterpark, Baku, with plenty of fun slides and a small zoo.

THE BASICS

✚ L1

✉ 36km (22 miles) north of Puerto del Rosario

🍴 Restaurants, cafés and bars

🚌 6, 7, 8

⛴ Ferry from Playa Blanca, Lanzarote (11–13 sailings daily; 20 min; ▷ 117)

Baku Family Park

www.bakufuerteventura.com

✉ Avda Nuestra Señora del Carmen 41

☎ 928 86 72 27

🕐 Daily 10–6 (closes earlier low and mid-season)

💲 Expensive

La Oliva

Sculptures at Centro de Arte Canario (left, right); Nuestra Señora de la Candelaria (middle)

THE BASICS

➕ L3

✉ 16km (10 miles) south of Corralejo

🍴 Café-bars

🚌 7, 8

La Casa de los Coroneles

✉ C/Coroneles

☎ 928 86 19 04

🕐 Tue–Sun 10–6

♿ Few 🎟 Free

Museo del Grano La Cilla

✉ Crta El Cotillo

☎ 928 86 87 29

🕐 Tue–Fri, Sun 9.30–5.30

♿ Few 🎟 Inexpensive

HIGHLIGHTS

- La Casa de los Coroneles
- Museo del Grano La Cilla
- Iglesia de Nuestra Señora de la Candelaria

TIPS

- Visit during the Fiesta de la Candelaria (2 Feb) to see this sleepy village come alive.
- To illuminate the elaborate church altar, drop a coin in the slot.

The pleasant, spacious village of La Oliva lies at the heart of an area with a rich past. On its outskirts is Fuerteventura's most impressive colonial mansion, which has been freshly restored.

Faded grandeur In the 19th century, La Oliva took over from Betancuria as Fuerteventura's social and political focus. This was a thriving farming area, its arid plain and barren-looking volcanic slopes producing cereals and pulses. In the 20th-century, the farming industry collapsed and La Oliva's mansions fell into disrepair, but restoration has brought some of them back to life. The most conspicuous central landmark is the church, Nuestra Señora de la Candelaria, whose imposing lava-stone bell tower can be seen from some distance. In the surrounding square, olive-shaded benches are arranged around a bubbling fountain.

Commanding residence La Casa de los Coroneles, the magnificent home of the island's 19th-century military governors, is occasionally used for art exhibitions and events. With fortress-like crenellations at either end, carved balconies along the façade and grandly proportioned rooms with polished wood floors, it's a swaggering edifice.

Agricultural heritage On the road to El Cotillo, just west of the church square, is the Museo del Grano La Cilla, a former tithe barn that now houses an agricultural museum. On display are old photographs and implements, with detailed descriptions of traditional farming methods.

Shaped like an outstretched foot, the Jandía Peninsula is a wild, rugged region of low, arid mountains and dunes, fringed on its southern side by stunning beaches of pale sand.

Blissful beaches It's these long, lovely beaches that make southern Fuerteventura such a powerful magnet for sunseekers and watersports enthusiasts. The resort towns of Costa Calma near the 'ankle' of the peninsula and Morro Jable at the 'heel' are both packed with modern accommodation complexes. They're unashamedly touristy but both manage to avoid the worst excesses of overdevelopment. Costa Calma has a gently curving, golden beach, while Morro Jable lies on the colossal Playa del Mattoral, where turquoise waters lap the shore and sunbathers stretch out under parasols. Both have clothing-optional areas. Morro Jable also has an old town—a ragged jumble of whitewashed buildings lining a ravine—and a port served by ferries from Gran Canaria and Tenerife.

Wild side In between is the magnificently unspoilt Playa de Sotavento, or leeward beach, backed by protected duneland. Here, at Risco del Paso, a sandbar creates a breezy tidal lagoon that's a perfect training place for windsurfers; you can watch their progress from the beach bar beside the windsurf station. The shallow Atlantic waters beyond are always busy with hardened enthusiasts testing their mettle, while on Playa Barca, a little to the north, you can watch kitesurfers perform gravity-defying freestyle moves.

THE BASICS

⊞ E9–G8

✉ Costa Calma and Morro Jable are 67km (42 miles) and 88km (55 miles) south of Puerto del Rosario respectively

🍴 Restaurants, cafés and bars

🚌 1, 4, 5, 9, 10, 25

🚢 Morro Jable to Las Palmas and Santa Cruz de Tenerife with Naviera Armas (www.naviera-armas.com)

♿ Few

HIGHLIGHTS

● Costa Calma
● Playa de Sotavento
● Morro Jable

TIP

● The annual Fuerteventura Windsurfing and Kitesurfing World Cup is held on Playa Barca over two weeks from mid-July.

Parque Natural de las Dunas de Corralejo

TOP 25

● Strolling over the dunes
● Flag Beach

TIPS

● For a beach with parasols and sunloungers, head for the northern part of the park, near the hotels.
● In the quieter areas away from the sunloungers, the coves and dunes are clothing-optional.

The dazzling drifts of white sand south of Corralejo are fantastic for swimming, kitesurfing or isolated strolling, and boast superb views across the Bocaina Strait to Isla de Lobos and southern Lanzarote.

Ancient sands Some used to speculate that Saharan winds might have carried the remarkably fine, pale sand that forms the Corralejo Dunes across to Fuerteventura's northeastern coast. But it's now generally accepted that the dunes were formed from ancient marine deposits, pushed or swept up from the ocean floor over millennia. Protected both for their natural beauty and as a breeding habitat for a rare desert-dwelling bird, the obarra, the dunes cover an area of 27sq km (10.5sq miles), and they also support unusual plant species that can thrive in these dry, salty

The incredible endless sand dunes at Parque Natural de las Dunas de Corralejo are not only littered with human explorers—expect to see a goat or two roaming the rolling dunes

sands. The area is within easy reach of the town of Corralejo by bus or on foot; two of Corralejo's most conspicuous hotels, which pre-date the creation of the park, lie within its boundaries.

Feel the breeze There's no gate to the park; a main road (the FV-1 to Puerto del Rosario) runs through it staying close to the shore, with plenty of space to park. On the inland side of the road creamy-soft dunes stretch far into the distance, while on the ocean side perfect little coves are separated by dark volcanic rock. It's generally safe to swim here, except on stormy days when the surf gets up. At the northern end of the park is a famous windsurfing and kitesurfing zone, Flag Beach, where you can sign up for lessons (▷ 104) or just watch the spectacle of racing sails and soaring kites.

THE BASICS

✚ L2

✉ 5km (3 miles) south of Corralejo

🚌 6

♿ None

✋ Free

More to See

ANTIGUA

Spread out across a broad valley in the middle of the island, Antigua is a placid town with a farming heritage, which is celebrated in its pleasant museum, the Molino de Antigua. Here you can climb inside a carefully restored *molino* (two-storey windmill), once used to grind grain into gofio. There's also an impressive cactus garden, plus an exhibition of artefacts relating to the indigenous islanders, and traditional crafts such as weaving and lace.

🖽 K5 ☒ 20km (12miles) southwest of Puerto del Rosario 🚌 1, 16

Molino de Antigua

☒ FV-20, 1km (0.6 mile) north of Antigua
☎ 928 85 14 00 🕓 Tue–Fri, Sun 9.30–5.30
🍴 Café 🚹 Good 🎟 Inexpensive

CALETA DE FUSTE

Locally known as Caleta but sometimes called (and signposted) El Castillo, after its small 18th-century coastal fort, this is a low-rise, middle-market, purpose-built holiday resort, whose most notable features are its golden beach and its 18-hole golf course (▷ 104).

🖽 L5 ☒ 14km (9 miles) south of Puerto del Rosario 🍴 Resort-style restaurants, cafés and bars 🚌 3, 10, 16

EL COTILLO

Once little more than a cluster of fishermen's cottages overlooking a pebbly cove on the breezy northwest shore, El Cotillo is growing; accommodation complexes have appeared near the calm lagoons on the north side of the village, and a mishmash of new buildings are springing up around the cove. For now, it's still a low-key place for a leisurely lunch of fresh-off-the-boat fish. An 18th-century turret on the cliffs, Castillo de El Tostón, houses art and photography exhibitions; local surfers ride the fierce waves nearby.

🖽 K2 ☒ 20km (12miles) southwest of Corralejo 🍴 Restaurants and bar-cafés
🚌 7, 8

Castillo de El Tostón

☎ 928 86 62 35
🕓 Jul–end Sep Mon–Fri 9–3; Oct–end Jun Mon–Fri 9–4 🚹 Few 🎟 Free

A beautifully restored windmill, the Molino de Antigua

Sunset at Caleta de Fuste

ECOMUSEO DE LA ALCOGIDA

This collection of traditional farm-houses, barns and windmills has been turned into an agricultural museum that conveys a strong sense of the hard graft that characterized the day-to-day lives of local farmworkers.

☩ K4 ✉ Near Tefía, 21km (13 miles) west of Puerto del Rosario ☎ 928 17 54 34 or 928 86 23 00 ⏰ Tue–Fri, Sun 10–6 🚌 2 ♿ Few 🎟 Inexpensive

LAJARES

This unassuming village is famous for its lacemaking—there is local work on show at the Escuela de Artesanía (▷ 102). Lajares lies at the foot of the impressive, russet-coloured Montaña de las Coloradas, near dramatic badlands strewn with ancient, lichen-covered lava. The area beyond was once rich farming country; a pair of restored windmills (a *molino* and a *molina*) stands on the road leading south out of the village.

☩ K2 ✉ 12km (7.5miles) southwest of Corralejo 🍴 Restaurant and café 🚌 7, 8

MONTAÑA TINDAYA

This ancient, extinct volcano, one of the most prominent features of the northern landscape, is thought to have been sacred to the indigenous islanders: podomorphs (rock art in the form of footprint-like symbols) and other ancient remains have been discovered there.

☩ K3 ✉ 24km (15 miles) southwest of Corralejo 🚌 7

MONUMENTO A DON MIGUEL DE UNAMUNO

Dwarfed by the sheer slope of Montaña Quemada, this solemn stone statue commemorates Miguel de Unamuno (1864–1936), the celebrated Spanish writer and republican activist. Unamuno was exiled on Fuerteventura for four months in 1924 after expressing his opposition to the then Spanish Premier, Primo de Rivera. He developed a great affection for the island's harsh simplicity, calling it 'an oasis in… the desert of civilization', a description Fuerteventurans

Podomorphs at the top of Montãna Tindaya

Typical example of an artisan's family house, Ecomuseo de la Alcogida

have dined out on ever since.
➕ K3 ✉ Near the FV10-FV207 junction, 24km (15 miles) southwest of Corralejo 🚌 2, 7 ♿ None 💶 Free

OASIS PARK

www.lajitaoasispark.com

Announced by a flamboyant display of flowers, this excellent attraction is part botanical garden, part zoo. Among the inspirational array of drought-loving plants is Europe's largest cactus collection: a surreal assortment of bulbous, spiky and furry specimens. The zoo features camel rides, aviaries and an African zone, home to giraffes, zebras, hippos and perky meerkats. Reptile keepers will offer to drape a python over your shoulders, and sealions perform hilarious tricks.
➕ H8 ✉ Crta Jandía, La Lajita ☎ 902 40 04 34 🕐 Daily 9–6 (to 7.30 in summer) 🍴 Restaurants and cafés 🚌 1, 10, 11, 25 ♿ Good 💶 Expensive

PÁJARA

Tucked into a valley among the island's most scenic highlands,

Pájara's village church is much admired for the unusual Aztec-like carvings surrounding its main entrance. Named Nuestra Señora de Regla after a town in Cuba to which several families of islanders emigrated during the 19th century, its statue of the Virgin—which has pride of place behind one of the altars—is also thought to be Cuban.
➕ J6 ✉ 44km (27 miles) southwest of Puerto del Rosario 🍴 Restaurants and bar-cafés 🚌 4, 9, 18

LAS PLAYITAS

Fuerteventura's latest resort development, adjacent to a very low-key village of the same name, offers upmarket accommodation, a new golf course and a full-sized Olympic swimming pool.
➕ K7 ✉ 45km (28 miles) south of Puerto del Rosario 🍴 Resort-style restaurants, cafés and bars 🚌 12

PUERTO DEL ROSARIO

Fuerteventura's capital is a working port that has plenty of authentic

Inside Iglesia de la Vírgen, Pájara (left); camels await their passengers, Oasis Park (above)

urban character but doesn't set out to draw tourists. On the central church square is the city's main visitor attraction, Casa Museo Unamuno, a small museum dedicated to the only famous literary figure with which the island has a significant association. Housed in the former Hotel Fuerteventura, where Unamuno stayed in 1924 (▷ 97), it displays a few period objects, and extracts from the poet's writings. The city also features a contemporary art centre, the Juan Ismael.

🕂 L4 ✉ 36km (22 miles) south of Corralejo 🍴 Restaurants, cafés and bars 🚌 1, 2, 3, 6, 7, 10, 14, 15, 16

Casa Museo Unamuno

✉ C/ Virgen del Rosario 11 ☎ 928 86 23 76 🕐 Mon–Fri 9–2 ⛳ Good 🎟 Free

Centro de Arte Juan Ismael

✉ C/ Almirante Lallermand 30 ☎ 928 85 97 50 🕐 Tue–Sat 10–1, 5–9 ⛳ Good 🎟 Free

VEGA DE RÍO PALMA

This pretty inland village is best known for its lovely little church,

Nuestra Señora de la Peña, which is the focus of an annual *romería* or traditional Catholic pilgrimage, held each September, followed by a grand fiesta in the church square.

🕂 J5 ✉ 34km (21 miles) southwest of Puerto del Rosario 🍴 Restaurant in the village 🚌 2

VILLAVERDE

On the fringes of this scattered inland village, in the north of the island, stand a couple of traditional windmills that have been carefully restored. There's also a geological site, the Cueva del Llano, which is the only large volcanic tube on the island. Inside the cave, researchers have discovered the fossils of extinct rodents and birds, plus a living endemic species, the spider-like *maiorerus randoi*. Guided tours operate every half hour.

🕂 L2 ✉ 13km (8 miles) south of Corralejo 🚌 7, 8

Cueva del Llano

☎ 928 17 59 28 🕐 Tue–Sat 10–6 ⛳ Few 🎟 Moderate

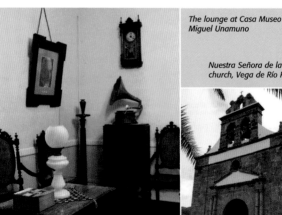

The lounge at Casa Museo Miguel Unamuno

Nuestra Señora de la Peña church, Vega de Río Palma

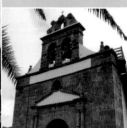

Exploring Northern and Central Fuerteventura

This complete circuit gives you a good overview of the island; you might then decide to explore in more depth on another occasion.

DISTANCE: 151km (93.5 miles) **ALLOW:** A full day

START .... END

CORRALEJO   **CORRALEJO**

① From Corralejo (▷ 90–91), drive south along the FV-101 to La Oliva (▷ 92). At the church, take the turning that heads to the east side of town to admire La Casa de los Coroneles.

⑧ Continue north along the FV-20 then turn onto the FV-207 for Tefia in order to retrace your route back to Corralejo.

② Leave La Oliva via the FV-10, heading south past Montaña Tindaya (▷ 97) and the Monumento a Don Miguel de Unamuno (▷ 97).

⑦ From Pájara, the FV-30 continues to Tuineje, where you should turn north onto the FV-20 for Antigua (▷ 96). The Molina de Antigua is on the way out of town to the north.

③ About 14km (8.5 miles) south of La Oliva, turn onto the FV-207 to Tefia, where you can visit the Ecomuseo La Alcogida (▷ 97).

⑥ Follow the FV-30 as it winds its way through dramatic mountain scenery to Vega del Río Palma (▷ 100). Carry on south to the leafy village of Pájara (▷ 99).

④ Drive south along the FV-207 then, 6km (3.5 miles) south of Tefia, turn onto the FV-30 to climb into the central mountains. Drop in at the Mirador de Morro Velosa (▷ panel, 88) for a drink.

⑤ Continue along the FV-30, past the two statues of the Guanche kings, to the historic village of Betancuria (▷ 88), a perfect stop for lunch.

Shopping

CENTRO DE ARTESANÍA DE MOLINO DE ANTIGUA

Stop to browse through the fine selection of locally-made craft items sold here, including rustic ceramics, lace and jewellery inspired by indigenous symbology.

✚ K5 ✉ FV-20, 1km (0.5 mile) north of Antigua ☎ 928 87 80 41 🚌 1, 16

CLEAN OCEAN PROJECT

www.cleanoceanproject.org
A range of cool casual clothing with a marine conservation message; there are also branches in Corralejo and Costa Teguise.

✚ K2 ✉ C/ Muelle de Pescadores, El Cotillo 🚌 7, 8

ESCUELA DE ARTESANÍA CANARIA

This is the island's largest selection of traditional handmade lace and crochet; you can sometimes watch artisans at work.

✚ K2 ✉ C/ Colonel González de Hierro 14, Lajares ☎ 928 86 83 00 🚌 7, 8

MYSTIC

Indulge in the masses of aloe vera products and herbal remedies, plus natural sponges and massage kits.

✚ g2 ✉ C/ Isla de Lobos 4, Corralejo ☎ 928 53 59 58 🚌 6, 7, 8

TIENDA DE ARTESANÍA

Authentic pottery, bags, jewellery, woven hats and oddments, made by Fuerteventuran artisans.

✚ J5 ✉ C/ Roberto Roldán 17, Betancuria ☎ 928 87 82 41 🚌 2

Entertainment and Activities

ANTIGUO CAFÉ DEL PUERTO

Harbourside bar with a mellow atmosphere, good for early-evening drinks and tapas.

✚ g2 ✉ C/ Ballena 10, Corralejo ☎ 928 53 58 44 🕐 Thu–Tue 10am–1am 🚌 6, 7, 8

BLANCO CAFÉ

This cool, glossy cocktail lounge and internet zone is a sophisticated newcomer to Corralejo. Settle yourself on a cushion and soak up the vibe. DJ sessions Saturday nights.

✚ g2 ✉ C/ Iglesia 27, Corralejo ☎ 928 53 65 99 🕐 Daily 6.30pm–2am 🚌 6, 7, 8

BLUE ROCK

Long-established Old Town bar hosting nightly live music from rock, blues and Celtic bands.

✚ g2 ✉ Corralejo ☎ 928

ON TWO WHEELS

The island government intends to build a network of cycle lanes that should, eventually, cover the entire island. At present, Fuerteventura's main roads include narrow stretches with blind corners, making cycling potentially hazardous. The new lanes will open up the dramatic interior to anyone fit enough to tackle its challenging gradients.

---

11 32 82 🕐 Daily 1pm–2am 🚌 6, 7, 8

CASA PRINCESS ARMINDA

www.princessarminda.com
Tranquil spot in an old family house with a sun-dappled courtyard. Try their special: a non-alcoholic cocktail of orange juice, pomelo, lemonade and grenadine. Also good tapas and occasional folk music.

✚ J5 ✉ C/ Juan de Bethencourt 2, Betancuria ☎ 928 87 89 79 🕐 Daily 11–11 🚌 2

CATAMARÁN CELIA CRUZ

This daily glass bottom

boat trip from Corralejo to Isla de Lobos, departs at 9.45am, returning at 2.20pm or 5pm, plus there are also one-hour cruises around the island daily leaving at 1pm, plus at 4.15 Mon, Wed–Fri and Sun.

🇭 h2 ✉ Puerto de Corralejo ☎ 646 53 10 68 🚌 6, 7, 8

CATLANZA

www.catlanza.com
This Lanzarote-based catamaran company (▷ 77) offers relaxing sailing excursions from Corralejo to Lanzarote's Papagayo beaches.

CORKY'S BAR

Run by a luminary of the Fuerteventuran surf scene, this is a good place to hang out with local wave-riders. Surfing videos on screen and live DJ and party vibe at weekends.

🇭 g3 ✉ CC Atlántico, Corralejo 🕐 Daily 11–late 🚌 6, 7, 8

DIVE CENTER CORRALEJO

www.divecentercorralejo.com
Established operator, running local trips daily except Sunday; the cool water around Corralejo ensures an interesting variety of marine life including angel sharks, rays, barracuda and bream. Offers PADI courses.

🇭 h1 ✉ C/ Nuestra Señora del Piño, Corralejo ☎ 928 53 59 06 🚌 6, 7, 8

FLAG BEACH WINDSURF AND KITESURF CENTRE

www.flagbeach.com
Northern Fuerteventura's leading centre, on the sands south of Corralejo, is a highly organized set-up, offering equipment hire and expert tuition at all levels. Island Boarders, who offer surfing training, are based here.

🇭 L1 ✉ C/ General Linares 31, Corralejo ☎ 928 86 63 89 🚌 6, 7, 8

FUERTE ACTION

This cool all-day bar and café attracts a broad mix of customers, which range from hardcore windsurfers to young families, with drinks, ice creams and light meals.

🇭 H8 ✉ CC El Palmeral, Costa Calma ☎ 928 87 55 13 🕐 Daily 8am–late 🚌 1, 4, 5, 9, 10, 25

WINDY SHORES

Fuerteventura's brisk winds blow all year round but are particularly strong in the summer, which makes it the best season for windsurfing and kitesurfing. The best waves for surfing, if you're confident, are in the wild northwest; El Cotillo is a popular spot. Swimmers should steer clear of the entire west coast, however, to avoid its treacherous currents: it's best to stick to the more sheltered beaches on the east and south coasts.

FUERTENDURO

www.fuertenduro.com
Jump aboard a 400cc Suzuki motorbike for an off-road tour. You're issued with a full kit including radio communication and a camelback of water. Beginners to experienced; pick-up service available.

🇭 K7 ✉ Gran Tarajal ☎ 646 65 64 93

FUERTEVENTURA GOLF CLUB

www.fuerteventuragolfclub.com
The island's original 18-hole golf course is a quality offering (par-70) with a driving range and a large putting green. There are also courses at Morro Jable, Las Salinas and Las Playitas.

🇭 L5 ✉ Crta de Jandía, Km 11, Caleta de Fuste ☎ 928 16 00 34 🚌 3, 10, 16

MUSIC BOX

Pulling in a healthy mix of locals and tourists, this club offers karaoke, Latin nights and live bands to keep the crowd happy.

🇭 g2 ✉ C/ General García Escamez 34, Corralejo ☎ 687 21 66 42 🕐 Daily 10pm–5am 🚌 6, 7, 8

PRO CENTER RENÉ EGLI

www.rene-egli.com
This well-known windsurfing and kitesurfing base is the epicentre of Fuerteventuran watersports culture. They stock large amounts of

equipment, suitable for all levels. International competitions are held in the vicinity.

🚩 H8 ✉ Hotel Sol Meliá Gorriones, Playa Barca ☎ 928 54 74 83 🚌 1, 4, 5, 9, 10, 25

PUNTA AMANAY DIVE CENTRE

www.punta-amanay.com
Professional outfit that specializes in trips to the Isla de Lobos. They also visit other sites near Corralejo, and run day trips to the wrecks near Puerto del Carmen. A

CARNAVAL

Island nightlife takes on a vivid hue during the pre-Lenten celebrations—don't be surprised if you come across gaggles of macho-looking locals dressed in drag, living it up in outrageous style. All are welcome at the costume competitions and pageants that take place in marquees set up in public squares: feathered and sequinned revellers strut their stuff, and jovial drinking continues late into the night.

nitrox facility is used, which enables divers to stay under the water for longer periods of time. PADI courses.

🚩 h1 ✉ C/ Pulpo, Corralejo ☎ 928 53 53 57 🚌 6, 7, 8

QUAD ADVENTURE

www.quadadventure.net
Explore the island's beaches, extinct volcanoes and dusty tracks by quad bike or beach buggy.

🚩 f3 ✉ C/ Bocinegro 17, Corralejo ☎ 928 86 65 52 🚌 6, 7, 8

Restaurants

PRICES

Prices are approximate, based on a 3-course meal for one person.

€€€	over €32
€€	€20–€32
€	under €20

BODEGUITA EL ANDALUZ (€€)

Cosy and upmarket little restaurant serving dishes from southern Spain, such as chorizo simmered in Jerez sherry, or lamb in thyme and Rioja sauce.

🚩 g2 ✉ C/ Ballena 5, Corralejo ☎ 676 70 58 78 🕐 Tue–Sat dinner only 🚌 6, 7, 8

LA CANCELA (€)

Pleasantly rustic pizzeria that produces juicy pizzas from its stone-fired oven.

🚩 K2 ✉ C/ Central 2, Lajares ☎ 928 86 85 68 🕐 Mon, Wed–Sun 5–11pm 🚌 7, 8

CASA MARCOS (€€)

This bar *gastronomía* is a fine, rural spot to enjoy classic tapas and wine. Folk musicians sometimes play on the terrace.

🚩 L2 ✉ Crta General 94, Villaverde ☎ 928 86 82 85 🕐 Mon–Tue, Thu–Sat lunch, dinner 🚌 7, 8

CASA SANTA MARÍA (€€€)

Wonderfully atmospheric

dining room in the heart of historic Betancuria, serving old-fashioned specialties such as roast lamb or kid. Though rather pricey, it's highly popular. Outside the restaurant is a café terrace bedecked with geraniums, serving good ice cream, coffee, cakes and snacks.

🚩 J5 ✉ Pl Santa María 1, Betancuria ☎ 928 87 82 82 🕐 Daily lunch, dinner 🚌 2

DON ANTONIO (€€€)

This excellent fine-dining village restaurant serves sophisticated fare such as delectable beef with rosemary and pine nuts in charmingly rustic surroundings. There's little

accommodation in this part of the island but it's worth a special trip.

➕ J5 ✉ Pl Virgen de la Peña, Vega de Río Palma ☎ 928 87 87 57 ⏰ Wed–Thu, Sun 11–5, Fri–Sat 11–10 🚌 2

EL HORNO (€€)

Within driving distance of Corralejo, this rustic restaurant has a great reputation for its traditional roasted and grilled meat dishes.

➕ L2 ✉ Crta General 191, Villaverde ☎ 928 86 86 71 ⏰ Tue–Sat lunch, dinner, Sun lunch only 🚌 7, 8

LA LAJA (€€)

With a great seafront position at the end of the promenade in Morro Jable's old town, this is a great spot to relax and enjoy local fish in less touristy surroundings.

➕ F9 ✉ Paseo Marítimo 1, Morro Jable ☎ 928 54 20 54 ⏰ Daily lunch, dinner 🚌 1, 4, 5, 9, 10, 25

MAHOH (€€)

This inviting rural restaurant with an impressive cactus garden has a blackboard menu of hearty fare, including tasty tapas and roasted pork or beef. Run by one of the island's ecotourism pioneers, it also has a few lovely guestrooms (▷ 109).

➕ L2 ✉ Sitio de Juan Bello, Villaverde ☎ 928 86 80 50 ⏰ Daily lunch, dinner 🚌 7, 8

THE POINT (€)

One of the most attractive of Corralejo's beach cafés, with a great timber deck overlooking Playa La Clavellina, and a mellow atmosphere. On the menu are healthy breakfasts and tasty salads and sandwiches, all at very reasonable prices.

➕ g4 ✉ Jardines de Hoplaco 1, Corralejo ☎ 608 72 25 41 ⏰ Daily 9am–10pm (to 9pm Wed) 🚌 6, 7, 8

POSADA DE SAN BORONDÓN (€€)

Atmospheric tavern with live Spanish music every night; fabulous, traditional tapas and main meals are served by friendly, hospitable staff.

➕ H8 ✉ CC Sotavento, Cañada del Rio, Costa Calma ☎ 928 54 71 00 ⏰ Daily 10am–2am 🚌 1, 4, 5, 9, 10, 25

ROQUE DE LOS PESCADORES (€€)

This first-class quality fish

GASTONOMÍA TIPICA

As on Lanzarote, for the best in local-style cooking, head away from the resorts to the inland villages and small coastal towns. Here, an increasing number of places are taking pride in producing authentic cuisine using island ingredients such as tomatoes, kid, succulent goat's cheese, octopus, squid and freshly-caught fish.

---

restauarant has a terrace with sea views. It offers a good range of local fare including snapper, mussels and langoustines, with delicious homemade desserts such as baked apples with vanilla ice cream to follow.

➕ K2 ✉ C/ Caleta 2, El Cotillo ☎ 928 53 87 13 ⏰ Daily lunch, dinner 🚌 7, 8

SIDRERÍA LA CABAÑA ASTURIANA (€€)

This unpretentious wharfside restaurant serves Asturian-style soups, stews and tortillas, with cider to wash it down.

➕ g3 ✉ Avda Marítima 3, Corralejo ☎ 928 86 75 22 ⏰ Wed–Mon lunch, dinner 🚌 6, 7, 8

TÍO BERNABÉ (€€)

Convivial restaurant in the heart of the Old Town, offering Canarian cuisine including goat stew, fried baby squid and *papas arrugadas con mojo*.

➕ g3 ✉ C/ Iglesia 17, Corralejo ☎ 928 53 58 95 ⏰ Daily lunch, dinner 🚌 6, 7, 8

LA VACA AZUL (€€€)

The best-located restaurant in El Cotillo, this relaxed place offers highly sophisticated and creative cooking from a Michelin-starred chef—the fish is superb.

➕ K2 ✉ C/ Requeña 9, El Cotillo ☎ 928 53 86 85 ⏰ Tue–Sun lunch, dinner 🚌 7, 8

These islands offer an impressive range of places to stay, from large family beach hotels to small inland retreats in converted *fincas*. With a little planning, why not spend part of your trip in a busy resort and part in the countryside?

Introduction	108
Budget Hotels	109
Mid-Range Hotels	110–111
Luxury Hotels	112

Introduction

On Lanzarote and Fuerteventura, most visitors stay in large complexes in the main resorts, where there are choices for every budget. It's common to book a package holiday but it's also easy to make your own arrangements.

Fewer in number, but excellent if you'd like to learn about the local way of life, are the islands' urban and rural accommodation options. In the capitals, there are a few untouristy urban hotels and *pensiones*, while in the inland villages you'll find delightful *hoteles rurales* and *casas rurales* (country hotels and guesthouses), often in beautiful converted historic buildings.

Lanzarote
Each of the three main beach resorts has a distinct character. Puerto del Carmen, the oldest, has a good variety of low-rise accommodation complexes—typically apartments sharing a pool—and bags of holiday atmosphere. Breezy Costa Teguise is a purpose-built resort that can't match Puerto del Carmen's village feel but is home to one of the island's best luxury hotels, alongside a sprawl of budget options. Playa Blanca is peaceful and pleasant and has the best range of modern resort accommodation for the relatively well-heeled.

Fuerteventura
Corralejo's Old Town makes it the most characterful of Fuerteventura's beach resorts, and low-key Caleta de Fuste is convenient for the airport and golf course, but most visitors head for the large hotels and apartment blocks of Costa Calma and Morro Jable.

ISLAND WATER

On the islands, tap water is desalinated; it's safe to drink, but its flavour and chemical content varies from area to area. Most prefer bottled water—local brands of still and sparkling are cheap when bought in bulk from supermarkets. Hotel buffets may include an urn of table water, but in restaurants it's normal to order water by the bottle.

Both islands offer a huge choice of accommodation, from large and luxurious to rural and charming

Budget Hotels

PRICES

Expect to pay under €90 per night for a double room in a budget hotel.

LANZAROTE

LANCELOT
www.hotellancelot.com
The best of the 111 rooms at this respectable, untouristy three-star city hotel have balconies overlooking Playa del Reducto. There's a rooftop swimming pool. Good buffet breakfast served in a room with seaviews.
➕ Off map at b1 ✉ Avda Mancomunidad 9, Arrecife ☎ 928 80 50 99

MIRAMAR
www.hmiramar.com
Brilliantly sited on the seafront at the heart of the shopping district, this is the most stylish of Arrecife's three-star hotels, with 85 simple but comfortable rooms; however, there's no pool.
➕ d2 ✉ Avda Coll 2, Arrecife ☎ 928 81 26 00

PENSIÓN CARDONA
www.hrcardona.com
This modest but well-kept city *pensión* has 60 ensuite rooms and is within easy walking distance of Arrecife's bus station, beach, shops, bars and restaurants.
➕ a1 ✉ C/ Dieciocho de Julio 11, Arrecife ☎ 928 81 10 08

PENSIÓN GIRASOL
A short stay at this simple, tidy little seafront guesthouse is the perfect way to enjoy the real La Graciosa—something the day-trippers miss. There's a simple bar-restaurant downstairs, and the beach is a few steps away. Low rates available, especially in winter. 11 rooms.
➕ F2 ✉ Caleta de Sebo, La Graciosa ☎ 928 84 21 18

PENSIÓN MAGEC
www.pensionmagec.com
Puerto del Carmen's only *pensión* is in a quiet part of the Old Town, but within ambling distance of the busiest bars and restaurants. It's very simple but clean and well looked after, with a choice of 14 shared-bathroom or ensuite rooms.
➕ D7 ✉ C/Hierro 8, Puerto del Carmen ☎ 928 51 51 20

BARGAIN BREAKS

It's often possible to find a cheap package holiday including resort accommodation at a rate that's low enough to fall within our budget bracket, but for the widest choice, try to travel outside peak season (Christmas, Easter, July and August). In quiet months, hotels may reduce their rates by up to 50 per cent, and package operators may throw in useful extras such as free or discounted car rental.

FUERTEVENTURA

CASA ISAÍTAS
www.casaisaitas.com
Charming and friendly village *casa rural* with just four ensuite rooms in an old country house. It has been lovingly converted by the present owners, who live on the premises. A delicious homemade breakfast is served in the pretty courtyard, and the attached bar-restaurant is a convivial spot for lunch.
➕ J6 ✉ C/ Guize 1, Pájara ☎ 928 16 14 02

ERA DE LA CORTE
www.eradelacorte.com
Fuerteventura's pioneering rural hotel is still one of the island's best. The house, which was built in 1890, has 11 rooms with plenty of character. The welcoming owners have enhanced the courtyard garden by adding a small swimming pool.
➕ K5 ✉ C/ La Corte 1, Antigua ☎ 928 87 87 05

MAHOH
www.mahoh.com
This delightful stone-built restaurant and guesthouse, created by a leading light in rural tourism, has nine ensuite rooms, some furnished with romantic four-poster beds. There is a pretty little swimming pool for total relaxation.
➕ L2 ✉ Sitio de Juan Bello, Villaverde ☎ 928 86 80 50

Mid-Range Hotels

PRICES

Expect to pay €90–€200 per night for a double room in a mid-range hotel.

LANZAROTE

EL ALJIBE

www.rural-villas.com

One of a small collection of beautifully converted self-catering properties in a quiet, rural area. This romantic two-person hideaway has a gallery-style bedroom over a cosy, rustic living space kitted out with most amenities.
🔹 F4 ✉ C/ San Isidro Labrador 12, Los Valles ☎ 902 36 33 18

CASA DEL EMBAJADOR

www.hotelcasadelembajador.com

An unexpected find in the heart of the fast-growing, modern resort of Playa Blanca, this elegant old seafront hotel with just a dozen rooms and a traditional feel. No pool, but there are good sea views from the terrace and it's very close to the beach.
🔹 B8 ✉ C/ Tegala 30, Playa Blanca ☎ 928 51 91 91

CASA TOMARÉN

www.tomaren.com

The young owners of this former *finca* near the edge of the Geria national park have lovingly converted it into six rustic self-catering villas, bohemian in style, which share a beautiful pool. The open landscape adds to the wonderfully peaceful, spacious atmosphere. Breakfast is included.
🔹 E6 ✉ C/ El Islote 33, San Bartolomé ☎ 660 40 40 79

CASERÍO DE MOZAGA

www.caseriodemozaga.com

Steeped in history, this small country house hotel oozes rural charm. Its eight rooms, arranged around courtyards, are decorated with interesting antique furniture and oddments. The attached restaurant is one of Lanzarote's best.
🔹 E5 ✉ C/ Mozaga 8, Mozaga ☎ 928 52 00 60

CASONA DE YAIZA

www.casonadeyaiza.com

In a grand country mansion dating back to 1825, this lovely boutique hotel is full of arty touches such as hand-painted

SELF-CATERING

Lanzarote and Fuerteventura have an abundance of mid-range self-catering apartments and villas that usually offer much more space to spread out than similarly priced hotel rooms. Most of them have use of pools; some also have delightful island-style cactus gardens. Supermarkets and restaurants are easy to find, which will leave you free to set your own timetable.

murals and elegant antique furniture. There's a small, unheated pool in the courtyard garden, and a top quality restaurant and gallery in the former wine cellar. Eight unique rooms.
🔹 B6 ✉ C/ El Rincón 11, Yaiza ☎ 928 83 62 62

CLUB LA SANTA

www.clublasanta.com

Catering specifically for sports enthusiasts, this large coastal complex offers basic accommodation and an action-packed activities programme. Its unbeatable facilities include gyms, pools, running tracks and a windsurfing lagoon; you can also borrow bikes, boats, kayaks, scuba kit and other equipment.
🔹 D4 ✉ Avda Krogager, La Santa ☎ 928 59 99 99

CORONAS PLAYA

www.coronasplaya.com

Efficiently run and spacious, this plain but spotless four-star hotel is particularly popular with British couples. There's a large pool area and Costa Teguise's beaches are within walking distance. A policy of not offering discounted rates for children ensures a calm atmosphere. 208 rooms.
🔹 F6 ✉ Avda del Mar 26, Costa Teguise ☎ 928 82 66 40

LOS FARIONES

www.grupofariones.com

The attractive seafront

pool terrace, shaded by leaning palms, and the unbeatable location close to the action in Puerto del Carmen, make this a popular choice even though the rooms are rather dated. 242 rooms.

🪧 D7 ✉ C/ Roque del Este 1, Puerto del Carmen ☎ 928 51 01 75

LA GERIA

www.hipotels.com
With 243 rooms, a bright, stylish lobby and a modern atmosphere, this hotel is at the quiet end of Puerto del Carmen, with views over Playa de los Pocillos from the pleasant pool terrace.

🪧 D7 ✉ C/ Júpiter 5, Puerto del Carmen ☎ 928 51 04 41

HESPERIA PLAYA DORADA

www.hesperia-playadorada.com
Close to the beach, kids' clubs and ice cream shops, this large 466-room hotel, though not the prettiest place on the south coast, is comfortable, convenient and a hit with families.

🪧 B8 ✉ Avda Papagayo, Playa Blanca ☎ 928 51 71 20

IBEROSTAR COSTA CALERO

www.iberostar.com
Sleek four-star hotel with a fresh, modern vibe, good food, stunning swimming pools and a great sense of space. Its thalassotherapy centre has a fantastic array of

pools, fountains, saunas and steam rooms, and is a destination in its own right. 350 rooms.

🪧 C7 ✉ C/ Alegranza, Puerto Calero ☎ 928 84 95 95

FUERTEVENTURA

BARCELÓ FUERTEVENTURA

www.barcelofuerteventura.com
With 462 rooms, this modern hotel occupies a large swathe of the Caleta beachfront, catering primarily for golfers and families; it also has a thalassotherapy centre and spa.

🪧 L5 ✉ Avda Castillo, Caleta de Fuste ☎ 928 54 75 17

IBEROSTAR PALACE

www.iberostar.com
Great for beach-lovers, this modern and generously-proportioned 437-room complex fronts

---

HOTEL BUFFETS

To cater for the tastes of considerable numbers of guests of different nationalities, the resort hotels offer self-service breakfasts; many also offer the option of a buffet-style lunch and dinner. As a rule of thumb, half-board or full-board deals at large, budget places tend to be poor value, but the quality hotels usually lay on extravagant spreads with enough variety to keep their guests interested throughout their stay.

---

straight onto the glorious sands of Jandía beach. Good-quality buffets are served in the large family restaurant.

🪧 F9 ✉ Urb Las Gaviotas, Jandía ☎ 928 54 04 44

LAS MARISMAS

www.lasmarismas.info
The position, handy for the Baku waterslides and amusements, makes this a good choice for families. The accommodation is spacious with kitchen facilities, and there is a basic restaurant and a children's play area. 232 rooms.

🪧 L1 ✉ C/ Huriamen, Corralejo ☎ 928 53 72 28

RIU PALACE JANDÍA

www.riu.com
Right on the beach, this 200-room hotel is a good option when staying in Jandía. The rooms come with a balcony or terrace, air-conditioning and minibar. Buffet meals are available (▷ panel).

🪧 F9 ✉ Playa de Jandía, Jandía ☎ 928 54 03 70

SOL MELIÁ GORRIONES

www.solmelia.com
On an isolated stretch of the stunning Jandía peninsula, but close to the resort facilities of Costa Calma, this 418-room hotel is a good choice for windsurfers, and is packed during tournaments.

🪧 J6 ✉ Playa Barca, Pájara ☎ 928 54 70 25

Luxury Hotels

PRICES

Expect to pay over €200 per night for a double room in a luxury hotel.

LANZAROTE

ARRECIFE GRAN HOTEL

www.arrecifehoteles.com
Controversial when built in the 1960s, Lanzarote's only tower block rises above it all with elegant public spaces and impeccable standards. Excellent value for five-star comfort. 160 rooms.

🚩 a1 ☒ Parque Islas Canarias, Arrecife ☎ 928 80 00 00

GRAN MELIÁ SALINAS

www.solmelia.com
Part-designed by César Manrique, whose wall sculptures adorn the lobby, this was Lanzarote's first five-star hotel, and it's lost none of its glamour. The tropical courtyard garden and fabulous pool have film-star appeal. 315 rooms.

🚩 F6 ☒ Avda Islas Canarias, Costa Teguise ☎ 928 59 00 40

GRAN MELIÁ VOLCÁN LANZAROTE

www.solmelia.com
This modern resort hotel was inspired by traditional village architecture, with a miniature man-made volcano adding a bizarre touch. The 266 rooms are decorated in cozy country style. First class catering.

🚩 B8 ☒ Urb Castillo del Aguila, Playa Blanca ☎ 928 51 91 85

HESPERIA LANZAROTE

www.hesperia-lanzarote.com
Dramatically modern and both spacious and intimate—each of the many pools scattered around the terraced garden has a private feel. Set apart on the edge of swish Puerto Calero, the atmosphere is exclusive; spa and wellness centre. 335 rooms.

🚩 C7 ☒ Urb Cortijo Viejo, Puerto Calero ☎ 828 08 08 00

LOS JAMEOS PLAYA

www.los-jameos-playa.de
This comfortable resort hotel, much influenced by the ideals of César Manrique, has a vast lobby styled like a grand Canarian mansion and beautiful gardens. The nightly buffet is deservedly popular. 530 rooms.

🚩 D7 ☒ C/ Marte 2, Playa de los Pocillos, Puerto del Carmen ☎ 928 51 17 17

PRINCESA YAIZA

www.princesayaiza.com
Right on Playa Blanca's pretty sandy beach, this is a brilliant option for families; with 380 generously-proportioned rooms and great swimming pools, plus a large children's activity and sports centre next door.

🚩 B8 ☒ Avda Papagayo, Playa Blanca ☎ 928 51 92 22

FUERTEVENTURA

GRAN HOTEL ATLANTIS BAHIA REAL

www.atlantishotels.com
Fuerteventura's most luxurious hotel is spacious, with sophisticated, Morocco-meets-Canaries styling and glorious views across the sparkling water to the Isla de Lobos. 242 rooms.

🚩 Off map at h5 ☒ Avda Grandes Playas, Corralejo ☎ 928 53 64 44

RISCO DEL GATO

www.hotelriscodelgato.com
Easily the most stylish and original place to stay in Costa Calma, this sleek hotel has 51 pod-like suites with circular bathrooms, a spa and a deliciously curvy pool.

🚩 H8 ☒ C/ Sicasumbre 2, Costa Calma ☎ 928 54 71 75

LUXURY VILLAS

For many, a villa makes perfect sense. A gorgeous, spacious pad with a private garden, pool and barbecue may cost no more than a top-end hotel room. One of the best options is Heredad Kamezí (🚩 B8 ☒ C/Mónaco, Playa Blanca ☎ 928 51 86 24; www.heredadkamezi.com), 31 beautifully designed, eco-friendly villas with maid service located a quiet stretch of the Playa Blanca seafront.

This section is full of practical information on planning a trip to Lanzarote and Fuerteventura, and finding your way around once you're there. As well as useful visitor information, we've included some language tips and historical pointers.

Planning Ahead   **114–115**

Getting There   **116–117**

Getting Around   **118–119**

Essential Facts   **120–121**

Language   **122–123**

Timeline   **124–125**

Planning Ahead

When to Go

The islands are popular winter-sun destinations for those from chillier climes. Spanish holiday-makers descend in large numbers in the hot, dry, windy months of July and August. Those wishing to avoid the crowds are likely to enjoy the quieter months of May, June, September and October.

TIME

Ⓛ Same as the UK–GMT, with daylight saving April to October; one hour behind mainland Spain.

AVERAGE DAILY MAXIMUM TEMPERATURES

JAN	FEB	MAR	APR	MAY	JUN	JUL	AUG	SEP	OCT	NOV	DEC
22°F	23°F	26°F	22°F	25°F	26°F	26°F	28°F	26°F	26°F	24°F	23°F
72°C	73°C	79°C	72°C	77°C	79°C	79°C	82°C	79°C	79°C	75°C	73°C

Spring (March to May) is breezy; temperatures are mild but unheated pools are usually too cold to swim in.

Summer (June to August) is dry and sunny; although the glare can be fierce, brisk winds usually keep temperatures moderate.

Autumn (September to October) is bright and mild; the sea is usually a pleasant 24°C (75°F).

Winter (November to February) brings occasional showers, grey days and cool evenings, but there's also plenty of sunshine; temperatures rarely drop below 15°C (59°F).

WHAT'S ON

January *Cabalgata de los Reyes Magos* (6 Jan): Epiphany street parades.

February *Nuestra Señora de la Candelaria* (2 Feb): Candelmas celebrations in La Oliva.

Carnaval (fortnight leading up to Shrove Tuesday): Costume parades, drag shows and fireworks.

March/April *Semana Santa* (date varies): Solemn Easter processions.

May *Fiesta del Trabajo* (1 May): Labour Day, with parades on the nearest Sunday.

Lanzarote Ironman (mid-May): Gruelling triathlon.

Día de Canarias (30 May): Archipelago-wide joyous celebration.

June *Corpus Christi* (date varies): Churchgoers decorate town squares with mosaics of coloured salt.

San Juan (24 Jun): Giant bonfires are lit the night before.

July *Nuestra Señora del Carmen* (16 Jul): Traditional music, dancing and wrestling in Teguise.

August *Fiestas del Carmen* (1–15 Aug): Parades, shows and a funfair in Puerto del Carmen.

Fiestas de San Ginés (1–31 Aug): Lanzarote's patronal fiesta, celebrated in Arrecife and all over Lanzarote.

September *Nuestra Señora de los Remedios* (8 Sep): Catholic pilgrimage in Yaiza.

Romería de Nuestra Señora de los Dolores (15 Sep): Pilgrimage and fiesta at Mancha Blanca.

Nuestra Señora de la Peña (mid-Sep): Fuerteventura's patronal pilgrimage and fiesta in Vega del Río Palma.

November *Lanzarote marathon,* Costa Teguise (late Nov/early Dec).

December *Christmas Eve* (24 Dec): Nativity plays and celebrations.

Lanzarote and Fuerteventura Online

www.cesarmanrique.com
Biographical information on Lanzarote's most famous public figure, with commentary on the inspiration behind his artistic creations.

www.centrosturisticos.com
Visitor information on Lanzarote's seven principal cultural centres from the Cabildo de Lanzarote (island government), including details of current exhibitions.

www.turismodecanarias.com
Official Spanish tourism website for the Canary Islands, with individual sections on Lanzarote and Fuerteventura and links to further websites.

www.fcmanrique.org
The site of the Fundación César Manrique, with reports in Spanish on recent and upcoming projects and events including exhibitions at the foundation.

www.fuerteventuraturismo.com
Clearly laid out site from the Fuerteventura Tourist Board, with useful information on museums and attractions, plus basic accommodation and restaurant listings.

www.gazettelanzarote.com
The best of Lanzarote's local magazines, published monthly, with informative features on local matters plus general interest articles, and an archive of past issues.

www.sunnyfuerteventura.com
Practical tips on life in Fuerteventura for visitors and residents. A useful site, though much of the information is irregularly updated.

www.turismolanzarote.com
A useful overview of the island and its attractions, including features on protected areas and rural tourism, from the Lanzarote Tourist Board.

GETTING ONLINE

Cybercafés are relatively rare on the islands, but most hotels provide broadband internet access via a few terminals (typically coin-operated, for around €4–€6 per hour) or WiFi (usually free) in their main reception area. The terminals are often much in demand so if you need to get online frequently during your stay it's useful to bring a laptop or other device. In the resorts, a growing number of bars and cafés offer free WiFi.

CYBERCAFÉS

Cybercafe Jable
➕ E5
✉ C/ Bernegal 4, Puerto del Carmen
☎ 928 59 60 01
🕐 Mon–Fri 8–3.30
💶 €6 per hour

Whereabouts
➕ d3
✉ Jardines de Hoplaco 10, Corralejo
☎ 928 53 54 18
🕐 Thu–Tue 10–10, Wed 10–3
💶 €3.60 per hour

Getting There

INSURANCE

EU nationals are entitled to emergency medical treatment on presentation of a European Heath Insurance Card (EHIC). Obtain one before travelling: the fastest method is to apply online at www.ehic.org.uk (UK citizens) or www.ehic.ie (Irish citizens). US travellers should check their health coverage before departure. In all cases, full travel insurance is still advised, particularly if your household insurance does not cover all the items you will be taking with you. If any of your possessions are stolen, you should obtain a police report from the Guardia Civil. Hotels and tour reps can provide an interpreter.

TOURIST INFORMATION

● Spanish Tourist Office www.spain.info; visits to STO offices must be booked in advance.
UK ☎ 020 7486 8077
USA: Chicago ☎ 312 642 1992; Miami ☎ 305 358 1992; Los Angeles ☎ 323 658 7188; New York ☎ 212 265 8822
● Turismo Canarias www.turismodecanarias.com

AIRPORTS

Lanzarote's international airport is Arrecife (ACE), 7km (4 miles) west of central Arrecife. Fuerteventura's international airport is El Matorral (FUE), 7km (4 miles) south of central Puerto del Rosario.

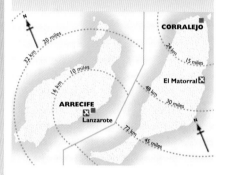

ARRIVING BY AIR: LANZAROTE

Arrecife airport, also known as Guacimeta (☎ 902 40 47 04, www.aena.es) is within easy driving distance of the capital and the island's three principal resorts: it's 7km (4 miles) from central Arrecife, 9km (5 miles) east of Puerto del Carmen, 33km (20 miles) northeast of Playa Blanca and 15km (9 miles) southwest of Costa Teguise. If you're travelling on a package holiday, you're likely to be transported to your accommodation by coach.

There's a cheap public bus service from the airport to central Arrecife that runs once or twice an hour between 7am and 10.25pm, but there is no public transport to the beach resorts. Taxis wait at the rank outside the arrivals hall; typical fares and journey times are: to Arrecife, €12 (10 minutes); Costa Teguise, €20 (20 minutes); Playa Blanca, €38 (30–35 minutes); Puerto del Carmen, €15 (10–15 minutes). Car hire firms with desks at the airport include Autoreisen (www.autoreisen.es), Cabrera Medina (www.cabreramedina.com), Cicar (www.cicar.com), Europcar (www.europcar.com) and Hertz (www.hertz.com).

ARRIVING BY AIR: FUERTEVENTURA

Fuerteventura's airport, El Matorral (☎ 902 40 47 04, www.aena.es) is 7km (4 miles) south of central Puerto del Rosario, 40km (25 miles) south of Corralejo, 8km (5 miles) north of Caleta de Fuste, 61km (38 miles) northeast of Costa Calma, and 82km (51 miles) northeast of Morro Jable.

Public buses run four times an hour from the airport to Caleta de Fuste (€1.30), Costa Calma (€6.50) and Morro Jable (€8.60). For Corralejo, you need to take a bus to Puerto del Rosario and change.

Taxis wait at the rank outside the arrivals hall; typical fares and journey times are: to Corralejo, €42 (40 minutes); Costa Calma, €66 (60 minutes); Morro Jable, €86 (80 minutes); Puerto del Rosario, €5 (10 minutes). Car hire firms with desks at the airport include Avis (www.avis.com), Cicar (www.cicar.com), Hertz (www.hertz.com), Payless (www.paylesscarrental.com) and Top Car (www.top-car-hire.com).

INTER-ISLAND TRAVEL

Two companies transport vehicles and passengers between Playa Blanca in the south of Lanzarote and Corralejo in the north of Fuerteventura. Naviera Armas (☎ 902 45 65 00, www.naviera-armas.com) makes seven sailings Monday to Saturday and five on Sunday (journey time 25 minutes); the price starts at €26.72 return for a foot passenger and €62.66 return for a car and two people. Líneas Fred Olsen (☎ 902 10 01 07, www.fredolsen.es) run a faster service that makes six sailings daily (journey time 15 minutes); prices are higher (ranging from €36.60 to €109.60 return). The first and last ferries from Playa Blanca leave at 7am and 7pm (both Naviera Armas); the first and last from Corralejo leave at 7.45am and 7pm (both Fred Olsen).

There are no domestic flights between Lanzarote and Fuerteventura, although Binter Canarias (www.bintercanarias.com) fly to the other Canary Islands.

ENTRY REQUIREMENTS

Lanzarote and Fuerteventura are part of the EU and holders of EU passports do not require a visa. Citizens of Australia, Canada, New Zealand and USA do not require a visa for stays up to 90 days. If planning to stay more than 90 days you must register in person at the local Foreigners' Office, and be issued with a certificate; the 90 days includes time spent en route through other Schengen zone countries. It is compulsory for passengers on all flights to and from Spain to supply advance passenger information (API) to the Spanish authorities—full names, nationality, date of birth and travel document details, namely a passport number. This can be done at the time of booking, or given to staff at check-in desks.

BAGGAGE ALLOWANCES

Budget and charter airlines flying into Lanzarote and Fuerteventura have strict weight limits on baggage; some charge a fee for every item you wish to carry in the hold, discounted if you book in advance online. Some allow only one item of cabin baggage per passenger. It's best to double-check before you set off for the airport.

Getting Around

MAPS

The free island maps and street plans available at tourist offices and hotel reception desks tend to be detailed and up to date. Recommended maps for those planning extensive explorations by car include those published by the AA (1:50,000). For hikers, the Lanzarote Tour and Trail map by David and Ros Brawn (1:40,000, Discovery Walking Guides) is indispensable.

BUSES

Each island has a daytime bus (*guagua*) network, which is cheap and reasonably efficient but more useful to residents than tourists, as most routes converge on Arrecife and Puerto del Rosario rather than linking visitor attractions. Many villages are only served by one or two buses a day, and bus stops are marked by small shelters. For timetables, visit www.arrecifebus. com (for Lanzarote) and www.tiadhe.com (for Fuerteventura) or check the local newspapers. On Lanzarote, the main terminus is on Vía Medular, Arrecife ☎ 928 81 15 22. On Sundays, direct services (Líneas 11, 12, 13) run from Costa Teguise, Puerto del Carmen and Playa Blanca to Teguise for the morning market. Fuerteventura's more useful routes include Línea 1, which connects Puerto del Rosario, Antigua, La Lajita, Costa Calma and Morro Jable once or twice an hour, and Línea 8 between Corralejo, Villaverde, La Oliva, Lajares and El Cotillo, hourly. Fares range from €1.15 for a short trip to €8.85 for Puerto del Rosario to Morro Jable, with concessions for under 16s, over 65s and students. Frequent travellers can save money by buying a pre-paid pass (called a *bonobus* on Lanzarote and a *tarjeta de dinero* on Fuerteventura).

DRIVING

Driving is the best way to explore, and practically essential if you decide to stay outside the main resorts. Car rental rates are very reasonable, particularly for extended periods (from €80 per week), but it pays to shop around. There are numerous offices in the airports and all the resorts. Drivers should carry their ID, licence and rental document at all times.

Rules of the road:

● Traffic drives on the right.
● The speed limit is 50kph (31mph) in urban areas, unless otherwise indicated, and 90kph (56mph) elsewhere.
● Look out for entry and exit ramps on the inside lane of dual carriageways, and left-hand turns that require you to turn into a right-hand

sliproad and stop before crossing the traffic.
● A no entry sign on the left-hand side as you exit a roundabout means stick to the right as traffic is two-way.
● *Cambio de sentido* on an exit sign means that the exit allows you to reverse direction by rejoining the road on the other carriageway.

TAXIS

Licensed taxis are metered and wait at ranks or can be hailed in the street. The sign on the roof is illuminated when the car is available. A short hop costs around €4–€6; a 20-minute journey around €25; plus supplements for airport trips. Taxi numbers include, on Lanzarote: airport ☎ 928 52 06 67; Arrecife ☎ 928 81 27 10; Costa Teguise ☎ 928 52 42 23; Puerto del Carmen ☎ 928 52 42 20; Yaiza ☎ 928 52 42 22. On Fuerteventura: airport ☎ 928 85 54 32; Caleta de Fuste ☎ 928 16 30 04; Corralejo ☎ 928 53 74 41; Jandía ☎ 928 54 12 57; Puerto del Rosario ☎ 928 85 02 16

LOCAL TOURIST OFFICES

The island offices and booths provide useful free maps of the islands and resorts, and leaflets on attractions. Most are open weekday mornings only, but the airport offices are open whenever incoming flights are due.
● Lanzarote www.turismolanzarote.com
Airport: Arrivals Hall ☎ 928 82 97 04;
Arrecife: C/ Blas Cabrera Felipe ☎ 928 81 17 62
Costa Teguise: CC Los Charcos 11 ☎ 928 82 71 30
Playa Blanca: El Varadero ☎ 928 51 90 18
Puerto del Carmen: Avda Las Playas ☎ 928 51 33 51
● Fuerteventura www.fuerteventuraturismo.com
Airport: Arrivals Hall ☎ 928 86 06 04
Caleta de Fuste: C/ Ruan Ramón Soto Morales 12 ☎ 928 16 32 86
Corralejo: Paseo Marítimo 2 ☎ 928 86 62 35
Morro Jable: Avda Saladar ☎ 928 54 07 76
Puerto del Rosario: C/ Almirante Lallermand 1 ☎ 928 53 08 44

PARKING AND FUEL

● Zigzags or solid yellow kerb markings mean no parking.
● Blue kerb markings mean short-term pay-and-display during business hours (kerbside ticket machines give details); free parking at other times.
● Broken white kerb markings or no markings at all mean free parking.
● Pay-and-display rates tend to be very reasonable (typically around €0.55 per hour). Private underground car parks charge considerably more.
● Most fuel stations on Lanzarote and Fuerteventura are not self-service; for lead-free, ask for *sin plomo*. It's usual to pay the attendant in cash. Fuel prices are lower than in the UK (around €0.95 per litre in 2008).

TOURS

Group coach tours, advertised in the resorts, can be a good way to get a quick overview of the islands' principal sightseeing spots without hiring a car. Most cost around €50–€60 for a full day and €30–€45 for a half day (children half price).

Essential Facts

MONEY

Euro notes come in denominations of 5, 10, 20, 50, 100, 200 and 500. Coins come in denominations of 1, 2, 5, 10, 20 and 50 cents and 1 and 2 euros. Credit cards are widely accepted although a few businesses (such as some petrol stations) require cash. ATMs with English language instructions are widespread and work exactly as you'd expect. Using ATMs to withdraw euros against your home account is generally cheaper than changing money at hotels or exchange bureaus, but your bank is likely to charge a flat fee per transaction, making it relatively expensive to withdraw small amounts.

5 euros

10 euros

50 euros

100 euros

CUSTOMS ALLOWANCES

● For customs purposes the Canary Islands do not count as part of the EU.

● The current limits on what you can carry to or from the islands without paying duty are: 2 litres still wine; 1 litre spirits or liqueur over 22 per cent volume or 2 litres fortified or sparkling wine; 200 cigarettes or 250g tobacco or 50 cigars; 60cc perfume; 250cc cologne or eau de toilette; gifts and souvenirs to a value of £145.

ELECTRICITY

● Current is 220 volts AC (50 cycles).

● The islands use standard European sockets for plugs with two round pins.

● Local electrical shops and hotel boutiques stock adaptors.

EMBASSIES AND CONSULATES

● UK: Edifico Cataluña, C/ Luis Morote 6, 35007 Las Palmas, Gran Canaria ☎ 928 26 25 08.

● Ireland: C/León y Castillo 195–1°dcha, 35004 Las Palmas, Gran Canaria ☎ 928 29 77 28.

● USA: C/Serrano 75, 28006 Madrid ☎ 91 587 2200.

EMERGENCY NUMBERS

● Fire, police and ambulance ☎ 112

MAIL

● Post boxes are yellow, marked Correos.

● A postcard to the UK/Europe requires a €0.60 stamp (*sello*).

MEDICAL TREATMENT

● All hotels have details of the nearest English-speaking doctor or dentist.

● For information on EHIC (▷ 116).

● Pharmacies (*farmacias*, indicated by an illuminated green cross) have well-informed staff.

OPENING HOURS

● Shops are typically open 9 or 10am to 8 or 9pm; many close 1–4 or 2–5.

● Post offices are open Mon–Fri 9–2 (some

have slightly longer hours).
● Banking hours are Mon–Fri 9–2, Sat 9–1.
● Most museums on Fuerteventura are closed on Sunday and Monday.

PUBLIC HOLIDAYS
● 1 Jan, 6 Jan, 2 Feb, 19 Mar, Maundy Thursday (Mar/Apr), Good Friday (Mar/Apr), 1 May, 30 May, Corpus Christi (May/Jun), 15 Aug, 12 Oct, 1 Nov, 6 Dec, 8 Dec, 25 Dec.

SENSIBLE PRECAUTIONS
● Crime is not a problem on either island. The greatest risk is theft by another tourist.
● Don't leave valuables on the beach or on show in a parked car.
● If your hotel room has a safe, use it for peace of mind.
● Fire is a risk in hotels—locate the nearest fire exit to your room and ensure it is not blocked or locked.

SMOKING
● Restaurants and bars display a sign indicating whether smoking is allowed.

TELEPHONES
● Mobile coverage is good but it's cheaper to use a public phone with a phone card (*tarjeta de teléfono*) from newsagents and travel reps.
● All phone numbers in the Canary Islands, have 9 digits; you must dial the whole number.

TELEPHONE CODES
● To phone the islands from abroad, use the Spanish code (0034).
● To phone abroad from the islands, dial the following code, then the number, omitting the first zero: UK 0044; Ireland 00353; Germany 0049; USA and Canada 001.

TIPPING
● Tips in restaurants, cafés, bars and for taxis, are normally rounded up to the nearest euro or, for good service, add up to 10 per cent.

MEDIA
As well as Spanish-language daily newspapers local to the islands, many newsagents, supermarkets and hotel shops stock current international titles, including daily papers and glossy magazines from the UK. Shops and bars distribute free English-language listings magazines with local features and property ads. The islands' English-language radio stations include Holiday FM (98.2 & 105.5FM), Power FM (91.5 & 91.7FM), QFM (98.0FM) and UK Away FM (99.9 & 99.4FM). Hotel televisions typically receive Sky and CNN plus several Spanish and German channels. Most towns and resorts have at least one bar where you can watch sporting fixtures on a big screen.

NEED TO KNOW ESSENTIAL FACTS

Language

The language of mainland Spain is Castilian, which is also carried over to the Canary Islands—although there are some differences in the pronunciation. Islanders don't lisp the letters 'c' or 'z', they are spoken softly. English is spoken in major resorts but if you intend to wander away from the tourist spots some basic Spanish would be useful. Below is a list of words and phrases that might help.

BASIC VOCABULARY	
yes/no	sí/no
I don't understand	no entiendo
left/right	izquierda/derecha
open/closed	abierto/cerrado
good/bad	bueno/malo
big/small	grande/pequeño
with/without	con/sin
more/less	más/menos
early/late	temprano/tarde
today/tomorrow	hoy/mañana
yesterday	ayer
good morning	buenos días
good afternoon/ evening	buenas tardes
good night	buenas noches
hello (informal)	hola
goodbye (informal)	hasta luego/hasta pronto
hello (answering phone)	Diga
goodbye	adios
please	por favor
thank you	gracias
you're welcome	de nada
how are you? (formal)	¿Cómo está?
how are you? (informal)	¿Que tal?
I'm fine	estoy bien
I'm sorry	lo siento
excuse me (in a bar)	oiga
excuse me (in a crowd)	perdón

NUMBERS	
1	uno
2	dos
3	tres
4	cuatro
5	cinco
6	seis
7	siete
8	ocho
9	nueve
10	diez
11	once
12	doce
13	trece
14	catorce
15	quince
16	dieciséis
17	diecisiete
18	dieciocho
19	diecinueve
20	veinte
30	treinta
40	cuarenta
50	cincuenta
60	sesanta
70	setanta
80	ochenta
90	noventa
100	cien
1000	mil

SHOPPING

ATM/cash machine	cajero
I want to buy...	quiero comprar...
do you have...?	¿tiene...?
blouse	blusa
dress	vestido
shirt	camisa
shoes	zapatos
skirt	falda
tie	corbata
small	pequeño
medium	mediano
large	grande
how much is it?	¿cuanto es?

EATING OUT

restaurant	restaurante
table	una mesa
wine list	la carte de vinos
smoking allowed	se permite fumar
no smoking	se prohibe fumar
menu	la carta
set menus	platos combinados
fork	tenedor
knife	cuchillo
spoon	cuchura
napkin	servilleta
glass of wine	copa de vino
glass of beer	caña
water (mineral)	agua (mineral)
still/sparkling	sin gas/con gas
coffee (with milk)	café (con leche)
May I have the bill?	¿La cuenta, por favor?
Do you take credit cards?	¿Aceptain tarjetas de crédito?
cakes	pasteles
small snacks	pinchos
sandwiches	bocadillos
set dishes	platos combinados
hot/cold	caliente/frío
I'd like...	me gustaría
desert	el postre
credit card	la tarjeta de crédito

FOOD

apple	manzana
banana	plátano
beans	habas
chicken	pollo
tuna	atún
duck	pato
fish	pescado
fruit	fruta
lamb	cordero
lettuce	lechuga
lobster	langosta
meat	carne
melon	melón
orange	naranja
pork	cerdo
seafood	mariscos
tomato	tomate

ACCOMMODATION

hotel	hotel
room	una habitación
single/double	individual/doble
twin	con dos camas
one night	una noche
two nights	dos noches
reservation	una reserva
rate	la tarifa
breakfast	el desayuno
bathroom	el cuarto de baño
shower	la ducha
balcony	el balcón
reception	la recepción
key	la llave
room service	el servicio de habitaciones

Timeline

FIERY ORIGINS

Lanzarote and Fuerteventura were formed by a series of volcanic eruptions that rocked this stretch of the Atlantic 17–20 million years ago. Subsequent eruptions created the other Canary Islands plus Cape Verde to the south, Madeira to the north and the Azores to the northwest.

Left to right: carving inside the 17th-century Cathedral of Santa Maria, Betancuria; a historic village sign, Betancuria; Monument de Unamuno, Tindaya; a watchtower on the sands at Playa Bastian, Costa Teguise; César Manrique Foundation, Tahiche; flags flying in the breeze over the town of Teguise

c2500BC The islands are settled by the Guanches, possibly Berbers from North Africa; Mediterranean-type Stone Age people who have no written language.

1300–1500AD Genoese and Mallorcan explorers visit the islands and map them; French, English, Dutch and Arab pirates raid them for slaves.

1402 Two Normans, Gadifer de la Salle and Jean de Béthencourt, sail south to tap the Saharan 'River of Gold' and convert non-believers to Christianity. They land on Lanzarote and claim the islands for their sponsor, the king of Spain.

1405 Béthencourt and de la Salle establish Betancuria, Fuerteventura's first capital.

1414 Foundation of Teguise, Lanzarote's first capital.

1730–36 Timanfaya blows its top and eruptions continue for another six years, destroying a third of Lanzarote's farmland. Many Lanzaroteans flee to Europe and South America.

1824 New volcanic eruptions on Lanzarote add more lava to the landscape.

1852 The Canary Islands are declared a free trade zone in an effort to boost the islands' economy.

1924 Don Miguel Unamuno is exiled to Fuerteventura for four months; he is much taken with island life and this influences his writings.

Early 1960s The first package tourists fly to the Canaries on holiday.

1966–1990 César Manrique creates a series of architectural installations on Lanzarote, starting with the Jameos del Agua and ending with the Jardín de Cactus. During this time, Timanfaya becomes a national park, and Manrique receives international awards for his conservation efforts.

1982 The sand dunes south of Corralejo and Isla de Lobos are made a national park by royal decree, confirmed by law in 1994.

1986 Canary Islands become full members of the European Community (as part of Spain).

1992 Lanzarote's first annual Ironman Triathlon takes place.

1993 UNESCO declares Lanzarote a biosphere reserve in recognition of the islanders' conscientious relationship with the natural environment.

2008 Celebrated Spanish filmmaker Pedro Almodóvar chooses Lanzarote as the location for his new movie *Los Abrazos Rotos*, starring Penélope Cruz.

EXPLORERS

Genoese sailor Lancelotto Malocello, who visited in 1312, is thought to have named Lanzarote after himself. The name Fuerteventura ('strong luck') is probably much older: the Greeks and Romans knew the Canaries as the Fortunate Isles.

GREEN ORIGINS

Fuerteventura was once a lush island: 14th-century Genoese explorers remarked on its abundance of goats and trees. In later centuries, over-grazing, deforestation and inexpert rainwater management caused rampant desertification to take hold, resulting in the parched, denuded plains and gullies we see today.

Index

A

accommodation 17, 107–112
aerial tours 78
air travel 116–117
Antigua 96
Aquapark 37
aquarium 37
Arrecife 8, 50–51, 71
Arrieta 36
ATMs 120

B

baggage allowances 117
Baku 18, 91
banana boat rides 63
banks 121
beaches 10
    clothing-optional 18, 36,
        93, 94
Betancuria 8, 88, 101
buses 118

C

cactus farming 30–31
Caleta de Sebo 32, 39
Caleta de Famara 38
Caleta de Fuste 96
Caleta del Mojón Blanco 36
camel rides 18, 59, 74
La Casa de los Coroneles 92
Casa Museo Unamuno 100
La Casa de los Volcanes 18, 29
Casa-Museo del Campesino
    17, 55
Casa-Museo Palacio Spínola 35
Castilla de Santa Bárbara 36, 41
Castillo de San Gabriel 50, 71
Castillo de San José 8, 52
caves 24, 100
central and southern Lanzarote
    47–84
    drives 73–74
    entertainment and activities
        76–79
    map 48–49
    restaurants 81–84
    shopping 76
    sights 50–70
    walks 71–72
Centro de Arte Juan Ismael 100
Centro de Arte Santo Domingo
    35
Centro de Visitantes e
    Interpretación 9, 17, 53,
        72, 74
Charco del Palo 18, 36
children's entertainment 18,
    38, 61, 91

climate and seasons 114
club scene 13, 76, 79
    see also entertainment and
        activities
Corralejo 9, 90–91, 101
Costa Calma 93
Costa Teguise 36–37
El Cotillo 96
crafts 12, 16, 42, 50, 102
credit cards 120
crime 121
cruises 11, 43, 79, 102, 104
Cueva del Llano 100
Cueva de los Verdes 9, 24
customs allowances 120
cycling 10, 102

D

disabilities, visitors with 118
drinking water 108
drives
    northern and central
        Fuerteventura 101
    northern Lanzarote 41
    Parque Nacional de
        Timanfaya 74
    southern Lanzarote 73
driving 118–119
dune buggies 79, 105

E

eating out 14–15
    Canarian cooking 14, 44, 106
    tapas 46
    see also restaurants
Echadero del Camellos 59, 74
Ecomuseo La Alcogida 97, 101
EHIC (European health card)
    116
electricity 120
embassies and consulates 120
emergency telephone
    numbers 120
entertainment and activities
    10–11, 13, 17
    central and southern
        Lanzarote 76–79
    Fuerteventura 102–105
    northern Lanzarote 42–43
Ermita de los Dolores 68

F

Femés 68, 73
fiestas and events 13, 32,
    65, 114
fire safety 121
Fuerteventura 4, 85–106
    drive 101

entertainment and activities
    102–105
map 86–87
restaurants 105–106
shopping 102
sights 88–100
Fundación César Manrique 9,
    18, 26–27, 41

G

goats, free-ranging 5
golf 37, 43, 99, 104
El Golfo 9, 54
La Graciosa 9, 32, 38
Guinate Parque Tropical 37

H

Haría 37–38, 41
Los Hervideros 68
history 124–125
hotels 17, 108, 109–112

I

insurance 116
internet access 115
Isla de Lobos 9, 89

J

Jameos del Agua 9, 18,
    28–29, 43
Jardín Botánico 18, 99
Jardín de Cactus 9, 18,
    30–31, 41

K

karting 77, 78
Kikoland 61
kitesurfing 11, 16, 38, 42, 43,
    93, 95, 104–105

L

lacemaking 16, 97, 102
El Lago (El Charco) de los
    Clicos 54
Lajares 16, 97
language 122–123
Lanzarote 4
    central and southern
        Lanzarote 47–84
    northern Lanzarote 20–46
Lanzarote Ironman triathlon
    10, 77

M

Manrique, César 5, 26–27, 28,
    30, 31, 33, 36–37, 38, 43, 52,
    55, 65, 68–69
maps, tourist 118

Marina Rubicón 61, 73, 76
markets 16, 34, 37, 38, 42, 50
medical treatment 116, 120
Mirador de Morro Velosa
  88, 101
Mirador del Río 9, 33, 41
Molino de Antigua 16, 96
money 120
Montaña Tindaya 97
Montañas del Fuego 59
Monumento al Campesino
  9, 55
Monumento a Don Miguel de
  Unamuno 97, 99
Morro Jable 93
motorbike rental 79, 104
Museo Aeronáutico 68–69
Museo Agrícola El Patio 9,
  56–57
Museo de Cetáceos de
  Canarias 69
Museo Etnográfico Tanit 70
Museo del Grano La Cilla 92
Museo Internacional de Arte
  Contemporáneo (MIAC) 52

N
nature reserves 11, 89
newspapers and magazines
  121
nightlife see entertainment and
  activities
northern Lanzarote 20–46
  drive 41
  entertainment and activities
    42–43
  map 22–23
  restaurants 44–46
  shopping 42
  sights 24–38
  walk 39

O
Oasis Park 18, 99
La Oliva 9, 92
opening hours 120–121
Órzola 38

P
Pájara 99
parasailing 63
Las Pardelas 38
Parque Nacional de Timanfaya
  8, 11, 18, 58–59, 74
Parque Natural de las Dunas de
  Corralejo 8, 10, 18, 94–95
passports and visas 117
Pedro Barba 39

Península de Jandía 8, 10, 93
personal security 121
pharmacies 120
Playa Blanca 8, 60–61, 73
Playa de las Conchas 39
Playa de las Cucharas 37
Playa Dorada 60–61
Playa de Famara 38
Playa Grande 8, 62–63
Playa del Mattoral 93
Playa Mujeres 64
Playa del Pozo 64
Playa de Sotavento 11, 93
Las Playitas 99
postal services 120–121
Pueblo Marinero 37, 43
Puerto Calero 69
Puerto del Carmen 13, 62, 69
Puerto Muelas 18, 64
Puerto del Rosario 99–100
Punta de Papagayo 8, 10,
  64, 73

Q
quad biking 79, 105

R
radio and television 121
La Reserva Natural Protegido
  de los Ajaches 64
restaurants 15, 16
  central and southern
    Lanzarote 81–84
  Fuerteventura 105–106
  northern Lanzarote 44–46
Risco de Famara 38
Risco del Paso 93
Ruta de Tremesana 17, 72
Ruta de los Volcanes 59, 74

S
sailing 11, 77, 79, 104
Salinas de Janubio 70
salt pans 70
San Bartolomé 70
sand dunes 18, 94–95
La Santa 70
scuba diving 11, 42, 63, 76,
  78–79, 89, 104, 105
self-catering 110
shopping 12, 16
  central and southern
    Lanzarote 76
  Fuerteventura 102
  northern Lanzarote 42
  opening hours 120
  sales tax 12

sightseeing tours 119
smoking etiquette 121
submarine safaris 79
surfing 11, 16, 38, 42, 43, 96

T
taxis 119
Teguise 8, 16, 34–35, 41
telephones 121
time zone 114
tipping 121
tourist information 115, 116,
  119
two-day itinerary 6–7

U
Uga 70

V
Valle de la Geria 8, 66–67, 73
Vega del Río Palma 100
villas 110, 112
Villaverde 100
volcanic landscape 4, 17, 18,
  24, 53, 54, 58–59, 72, 74, 97

W
walking and hiking 11, 78, 89
walks
  Arrecife 71
  La Graciosa 39
  Ruta de Tremesana 72
waterparks 18, 37, 91
websites 115
wind mobiles 26, 41
windsurfing 10–11, 16, 43, 93,
  95, 104–106
wines and wineries 12, 14, 56,
  66–67, 76, 82
wrestling, Canarian 34

Y
Yaiza 8, 65

Z
zoos 37, 91, 99

TWINPACK
Lanzarote and Fuerteventura

WRITTEN BY Emma Gregg
VERIFIED BY Penny Phenix and Hilary Weston
COVER DESIGN AND DESIGN WORK Jacqueline Bailey
INDEXER Marie Lorimer
IMAGE RETOUCHING AND REPRO Sarah Montgomery, Michael Moody and James Tims
PROJECT EDITOR Apostrophe S Limited
SERIES EDITOR Cathy Harrison

© **AA MEDIA LIMITED 2010**

Colour separation by AA Digital Department
Printed and bound by Leo Paper Products, China

A CIP catalogue record for this book is available from the British Library.

ISBN 978-0-7495-6152-9

Published by AA Publishing, a trading name of AA Media Limited, whose registered office is Fanum House, Basing View, Basingstoke, Hampshire RG21 4EA. Registered number 06112600.

Front cover image: AA/C Sawyer
Back cover images: (i) and (iv) AA/J Tims; (ii) AA/C Sawyer; (iii) AA/S Day

A03639
Maps in this title produced from mapping © KOMPASS GmbH, A-6063 Rum, Innsbruck

The Automobile Association would like to thank the following photographers, companies and picture libraries for their assistance in the preparation of this book.

Abbreviations for the pictures credits are as follows – (t) top; (b) bottom; (c) centre; (l) left; (r) right; (AA) AA World Travel Library.